Grammar Works
Student's Book 2

Mick Gammidge

CAMBRIDGE
UNIVERSITY PRESS

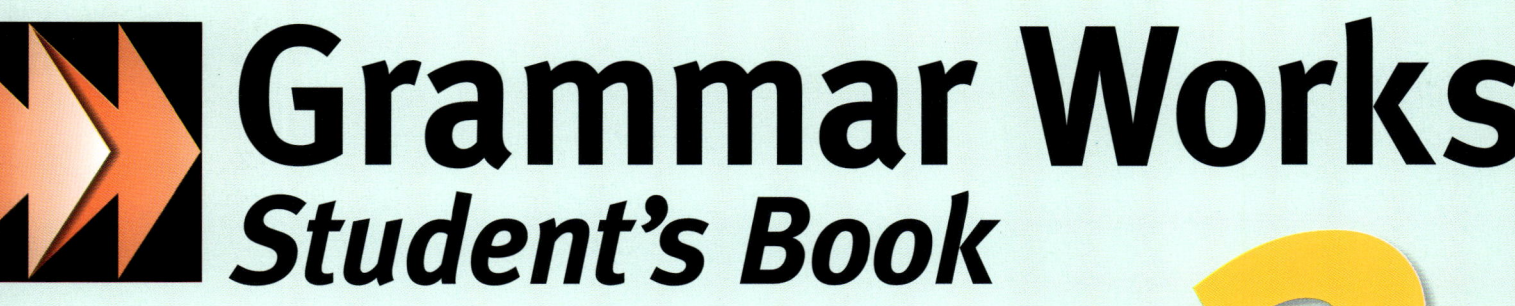

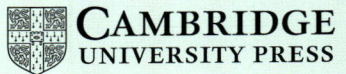

PUBLISHED BY THE PRESS SYNDICATE OF THE UNIVERSITY OF CAMBRIDGE
The Pitt Building, Trumpington Street, Cambridge CB2 1RP, United Kingdom

CAMBRIDGE UNIVERSITY PRESS
The Edinburgh Building, Cambridge CB2 2RU, United Kingdom
40 West 20th Street, New York, NY 10011-4211, USA
10 Stamford Road, Oakleigh, Melbourne 3166, Australia

© Cambridge University Press 1998

First published 1998

This book is in copyright. Subject to statutory exception
and to the provisions of relevant collective licensing agreements,
no reproduction of any part may take place without
the written permission of Cambridge University Press.

Printed in Italy by G. Canale & C. S.p.A. - Borgaro T.se (Turin)

ISBN 0 521 55541 8 Student's Book
ISBN 0 521 62625 0 Teacher's Book

Contents

Unit		Page
1	**Are you lazy or hardworking?** review: present simple, *have got*	4
2	**What are they thinking about?** review: present continuous	6
3	**We're going to start a band** review: *going to*	8
4	**Did Columbus find the East?** review: past simple	10
5	**Move slowly and carefully** adverbs of manner	12
6	**Missing meals is bad for you** gerunds	14
	Check point 1 – 6	16
7	**Will you go to Mars?** future *will*	18
8	**We shouldn't waste energy** *should*	20
9	**Are you doing anything next Saturday?** present continuous with future meaning; *nobody*, *something*, *anywhere*	22
10	**There aren't enough girls** countable and uncountable nouns; *too (much/many)*, *enough*, *not enough*	24
11	**The biggest in the world!** comparative and superlative adjectives; *as … as*, *not as … as*, *… than*	26
12	**It's the best!** comparative and superlative adjectives with *more* and *most*	28
	Check point 7 – 12	30
13	**It was rising from the sea** past continuous affirmative and negative; past simple contrast with *while/when*	32
14	**Which one was driving?** past continuous question forms; *which … ?*; *one/ones*	34
15	**He is the pilot that built the smallest plane** relative pronouns *who*, *which*, *that* in defining relative clauses	36
16	**I really enjoyed myself** Reflexive and emphatic pronouns; *each other*	38
17	**I used to forget everything!** *used to* affirmative, negative and question forms	40
18	**I won't be able to live without you** *could/couldn't*; *will/won't be able to*	42
	Check point 13 – 18	44
19	**Smith asked her where the robot was** reported speech	46
20	**You must come home at 10.30** *must*; *have to*; *can* for permission	48
21	**The work has been hard** present perfect simple affirmative and negative; *just*, *already*, *yet*	50
22	**Where have you put the chocolates?** present perfect simple question forms; *ever … ?*	52
23	**If he isn't fit, he won't play in the big match** first conditional	54
24	**Honey is eaten everywhere** passive – present and past simple	56
	Check point 19 – 24	58
	Grammar reference	60
	Wordlist	77
	Thanks and acknowledgements	80

1 Are you lazy or hardworking?

1a Read Sue's letter to her pen friend.

b Write the names of the people in the photo.

> In the photo, you can see me and my three friends. The tall boy is Paulo. He loves sport, but he doesn't like studying!
>
> The boy behind me is James. He's clever and hardworking. He studies science. He's got a telescope, so he can look at the stars. He only watches science programmes on TV!
>
> Kim's an interesting person. She plays the drums. I don't play a musical instrument, but I want lessons. I love guitar music, so I want a guitar.
>
> What about you? Do you like music too? Do you play an instrument? Do you like school? Are you lazy or hardworking? What do you do in your free time?

1 _____ 2 _____ 3 _____ 4 _____

2 Find sentences with **and**, **but**, **or**, **so** in Sue's letter. What do the words mean? Now put **and**, **but**, **or**, **so** in the sentences below.

1 The two boys are James _____ Paulo.
2 Sue loves music, _____ she doesn't play an instrument.
3 Is he James _____ Paulo?
4 He likes science, _____ he watches science programmes.

3a Complete the charts with the present simple.

+ affirmative

I _play_ an instrument.
She _____

– negative

I _____ an instrument.
She _____

? question

_____ you _____ an instrument?
_____ she _____

b Find the **-s** forms of the verbs below in Sue's letter.

1 love _____   3 watch _____
2 study _____ 4 play _____

c Now write the **-s** form of the verbs below.

1 teach _____ 3 stay _____
2 carry _____ 4 like _____

 CHECK YOUR ANSWERS AND STUDY THE INFORMATION ON PAGE 60.

4 Make one sentence from two sentences. Use **and**, **but**, **or**, **so**.

1 Are you lazy? Are you hardworking?
   Are you lazy or hardworking?
2 He hasn't got a bike. He walks to school.
3 Is it raining? Is it snowing?
4 He's got a broken leg. He can't play football.
5 I'm small. I'm strong.
6 She studies music. She plays the piano.

5 Complete the letter to *Alive* magazine. Use the verbs below.

~~be~~   be   don't like   hate   have got
keep   live   love   watch   write

Hi! My name ___is___ (1) Rhian.
I _____ (2) thirteen years old.
I _____ (3) on a farm in Wales. We
_____ (4) cows and sheep, and I
_____ (5) a pet rabbit and a hamster.
In my free time I _____ (6) TV and
_____ (7) short stories. I
(8) music and dancing. I _____ (9)
homework, I _____ (10) it!
Please write and send a photo.

6 Write questions for the answers below about the letter in exercise 5.

1 What is her name?
   Her name is Rhian.
2 _____
   She's thirteen years old.
3 _____
   She lives in Wales.
4 _____
   She watches TV and writes short stories.
5 _____
   Yes, she does. She likes animals.
6 _____
   She's got two – a rabbit and a hamster.
7 _____
   No, she doesn't! She hates it!

7 Look at the questions in exercise 6. Change the answers and write a letter about you.

Hi! I'm _____

PUZZLE

Tim always goes to school by bus. He often looks out of the bus window on his left, and he sees four pet shops. At night, on the way home, he sees four pet shops on his right. How many pet shops are there?

2 What are they thinking about?

1a Look at the painting. Read the text about it.

'The Last of England'
by Ford Madox Brown

People always ask questions about this painting. What is happening in the picture?
   The man and the woman are sitting on a ship, but where are they going? Are they coming home, or is the ship sailing away? In front of them, there is food for a long journey.
   Look at the woman's hands. Whose hand is she holding? Her baby is lying under her coat!
   Are they beginning a new life? Why are they sad? They're not looking at the passengers on the ship. What are they looking at? What are they thinking about?

b What do you think? Write **I think that / I don't think that** below.

1 _____ the ship is sailing away.
2 _____ they are beginning a new life.

2a Look at the text again. Put the words below in the correct order and make present continuous sentences.

1 | they | sitting | are | on a ship |
_____

2 | looking | aren't | they |
_____

3 | ? | the ship | sailing away | is |
_____

4 | they | are | what | thinking | ? |
_____

b Now put these words in the correct order and make present continuous sentences.

1 | she | holding her baby's hand | is |
_____

2 | aren't | the man and woman | waving |
_____

3 | ? | is | sleeping | the baby |
_____

4 | are | they | going | where | ? |
_____

3a Find the -ing forms of the verbs below in the text in exercise 1.

1 look _____   3 lie _____
2 come _____   4 sit _____

b Now write the -ing forms of the verbs below.

1 drive _____   3 jump _____
2 die _____   4 run _____

CHECK YOUR ANSWERS AND STUDY THE INFORMATION ON PAGES 60–61.

4 Look at the pictures. What is wrong? Use the verbs below and complete the sentences.

1 eat 2 listen 3 lie 4 take 5 walk

1 _She's eating_ a sandwich.
2 _____ to the teacher.
3 _____ down.
4 _____ a photo.
5 _____ on the grass.

5 Complete Sue's conversation with her little sister.

SUE: What _are_ you _doing_? (1 do)
MAY: I _____ (2 paint) a picture of a girl. She _____ (3 walk) in the park.
SUE: Oh, I see. _____ she _____ ? (4 cry)
MAY: No, _____ . She _____ . (5 shout)
SUE: Why _____ she _____ ? (6 shout)
MAY: Because her dogs _____ (7 run) away. They _____ (8 chase) a big dog.
SUE: Ah! Is this the big dog?
MAY: No! That's a woman! She _____ (9 look) for the girl. Are you stupid, Sue?

6 Complete the text. Use the present simple or the present continuous. Use the negative form once.

Paulo's uncle _is_ (1 be) a house painter, but today he _____ (2 work). He _____ (3 take) a holiday. He _____ (4 visit) the zoo because he _____ (5 enjoy) painting the animals. He _____ (6 sit) in front of the gorillas and _____ (7 draw) the babies. The babies _____ (8 play), but the mother gorilla _____ (9 watch) him!

7 Answer the questions about you.

1 Do you sometimes paint pictures?
_____
2 Are you painting now?
_____
3 What are you wearing?
_____
4 Do you always wear a uniform at school?
_____
5 What are you doing?
_____

PUZZLE

A boy is sitting on the right of a girl. A girl is sitting on the right of a girl. Two girls are sitting on the left of a boy. How many people are there?
_____

3 We're going to start a band

1a Read the conversation.

- When is your birthday, Sue?
- Next Tuesday.
- What are you going to get for your birthday?
- I'm going to start piano lessons.
- Yes, she's going to learn the piano, and then we're going to start a band. We're going to buy some new clothes, and we're going to dye our hair!
- I'm *not* going to dye my hair!

b Answer the questions

1 Does Sue study the piano? _____
2 Is she happy about Kim's plans? _____

2 Look at the conversation again. Complete the sentences with **going to** in the affirmative (+), negative (−) and question forms.

+	She 's going to get a present.	They _____ buy some new clothes.
−	She _____ dye her hair.	He _____ start piano lessons.
?	____ she ____ dye her hair?	____ they ____ start a band?

▶▶ CHECK YOUR ANSWERS AND STUDY THE INFORMATION ON PAGES 61–62.

3 In Britain, students choose some of their exam subjects. These are some students' choices for their exam subjects next year.

CLASS ...3B. SUBJECTS NEXT YEAR	Physics	Biology	French	Music	Art	Literature
Ann Jones		✓			✓	
Ben Smith			✓			
Liz Brown				✓		
Abdul Khan	✓		✓			
Tansy Lee				✓		✓
Tim North	✓					
Sue Bates	✓					

What are the students' plans? Choose from the list of jobs below.

artist   doctor   interpreter   musician   scientist   writer

1 Ann 's going to be a doctor.
2 Ben _____
3 Liz _____
4 Abdul and Sue _____
5 Tansy _____
6 Tim _____

4 Now look at the information in exercise 3 again and write sentences about the students' study plans.

1 Ann's going to study biology. She's not going to study music.
2 Ben ___
3 Liz ___
4 Abdul and Sue ___
5 Tansy ___

5 Read the conversation in exercise 1 again. Write questions.

buy   dye   get   learn   start

1 Is Sue going to get a present?
Yes, she is.
2 ___
The piano.
3 ___
A band.
4 ___
New clothes.
5 ___
No, Sue is not!

6 At New Year, British people make plans (resolutions) about things they are going to do or not do next year. Complete the conversation. Use the present simple, the present continuous or **going to**.

KIM: What ___are you doing___ (1 do), Sue?
SUE: Hi, Kim. I ___ (2 write) a list.
KIM: What ___ (3 be) it?
SUE: My New Year's resolutions. I always ___ (4 argue) with my little sister. I ___ (5 stop). And I ___ (6 bite) my finger nails. And I ___ (7 practise) the piano every day. ___ you ___ (8 have got) any resolutions?
KIM: Well, I usually ___ (9 eat) junk food, but next year I ___ (10 eat) healthy food. I ___ (11 do) my homework. Oh, yes! I ___ (12 forget) friends' birthdays.
SUE: Oh, good! When ___ (13 be) mine?
KIM: Er?

7 Write a list of your resolutions for next year.

PUZZLE

Sue is going to cut her birthday cake. She's going to cut the cake into five pieces with three straight cuts. Every piece is going to have two cherries. Where is she going to cut the cake? Draw the cuts.

4 Did Columbus find the East?

Christopher Columbus was an Italian from Genoa. In 1476 he moved to Portugal. He lived in Lisbon and made maps. He read about Marco Polo's visit to China, and he knew that the Earth was round. So he thought 'I can sail West and find the East!'

In 1492 Columbus sailed three Spanish ships – the Nina, the Pinta and the Santa Maria – across the Atlantic Ocean. Why did he take Spanish ships?

The Portuguese didn't believe him. So Columbus asked Queen Isabella of Spain for money and ships, and after five years, she agreed.

Did Columbus find the East? No he didn't, but he found the Caribbean Islands, and then South America.

1a Read the text about Columbus.

b Find ten past simple affirmative forms in the text. List them below and write their infinitive.

1 moved — move
2 _____
3 _____
4 _____
5 _____
6 _____
7 _____
8 _____
9 _____
10 _____

2a Complete the sentences from the text in the past simple affirmative(+), negative(–) and question forms.

+ He _____ in Lisbon.
– The Portuguese _____ _____ him.
? _____ Columbus _____ the East?
Why _____ he _____ Spanish ships?

b Now put the words in the correct order and make sentences.

+ [he] [South America] [found]
_____

– [didn't] [he] [East] [sail]
_____

? [sail] [he] [did] [West]
_____ ?

[he] [live] [did] [where]
_____ ?

3 Look at the pictures and write sentences about James's visit to a museum. Use the verbs below.

enjoy   go   leave   see   travel   visit

1 Last Saturday, James __visited__ a museum.
2 _____ with his father.
3 _____ by train.
4 _____ the Caribbean History room.
5 _____ at 5.30.
6 _____ his day.

CHECK YOUR ANSWERS AND STUDY THE INFORMATION ON PAGES 62–63.

4 Look at the pictures and write positive or negative sentences about James's visit. Use the verbs below.

see   watch   read   buy   ~~go~~

1 James didn't go to the restaurant.
2 _____
3 _____
4 _____
5 _____

6 Complete the information from the Caribbean Room at the museum. Use the verbs below and the past simple or the present simple.

be   be   be   build   build   ~~find~~   fish
give   give   grow   live   live   live
make   meet   speak   speak   speak

Columbus (1) __found__ the Caribbean islands in 1492. About 400,000 people (2) _____ there; the Arawaks and the Caribs. These people (3) _____ boats and (4) _____ for food.

First, Columbus (5) _____ the Arawaks on the Bahamas. The Arawaks (6) _____ Spanish, and Columbus (7) _____ the Arawak language. But the Arawaks (8) _____ very friendly. Columbus (9) _____ them presents, and they (10) _____ him and his men food.

The Arawaks (11) _____ good farmers. They (12) _____ corn, sweet potatoes, beans and other vegetables. They (13) _____ tools from stone, shells and bone. They (14) _____ small houses from wood and (15) _____ in villages.

Today, there (16) _____ 260,000 people on the Bahamas. Many people (17) _____ in towns, and they usually (18) _____ English.

5 Later, Paulo is asking James about his visit to the museum. Use the answers in exercise 3 to write Paulo's questions. Use the words below.

Did   How   What   ~~What~~   When   Who

1 What did you visit?
2 _____
3 _____
4 _____
5 _____
6 _____

7 Do you visit places? Look at the questions in exercise 5 again and write about your last visit.

I _____
_____
_____
_____

PUZZLE

I went to New York and stopped. I came back because I didn't go. What am I?

5 Move slowly and carefully

There are three types of owl in Britain: the Tawny Owl, the Barn Owl and the Little Owl. They all have good eyes. They also hear well and fly silently because they hunt with their ears. Little Owls can run fast too, but they look very strange.

Tawny Owl
Place ....
Date ....

Barn Owl
Place ....
Date ....

Tawny Owls and **Barn Owls** hunt at night, so you don't often see them. **Little Owls** hunt in the day too, so you can see them easily.

Owl Watching
- Move slowly and carefully.
- Speak quietly.
- Sit comfortably. Relax and wait patiently!

Little Owl
Place ....
Date ....

1a Read the information about owls.

b Answer **yes** or **no**.
1 Do owls have good ears? _____
2 Are owls quiet? _____
3 Are Little Owls slow runners? _____

2 Look at the adjectives below. Find their adverbs in the text.

Adjectives	Adverbs
careful	carefully
comfortable	
easy	
fast	
good	
patient	
quiet	
silent	
slow	

3 Look at the different spellings for the adjectives and adverbs in exercise 2. Write the adverbs for the adjectives below.

1 busy _____   happy _____
2 dangerous _____   brave _____
3 beautiful _____   special _____
4 simple _____   gentle _____

4a Write adverbs for the adjectives below.

fast fast   noisy _____
good _____   silent _____
high _____   slow _____

b Now write sentences about the pictures. Use the adverbs above and the verbs below.

climb eat fly move run walk

1 Cheetahs run fast.
2 Eagles _____
3 Tortoises _____
4 Pigs _____
5 Snakes _____
6 Monkeys _____

CHECK YOUR ANSWERS AND STUDY THE INFORMATION ON PAGE 63.

5 Look at the sentences with adjectives. Rewrite them with adverbs.

1 She's a careful driver.
  She drives carefully.

2 He was a bad painter.
  _____

3 They are loud singers.
  _____

4 He was a good actor.
  _____

5 They're noisy eaters.
  _____

6 She's a fast rider.
  _____

7 He's a hard worker.
  _____

8 She's a terrible writer.
  _____

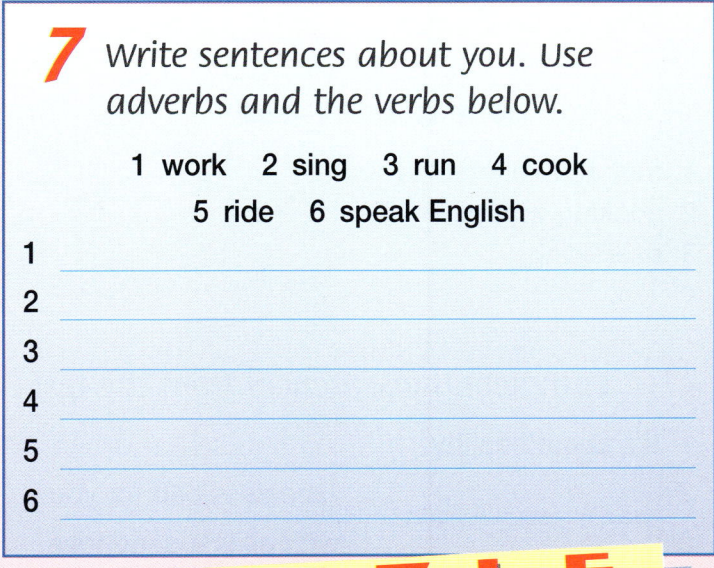

9 He's an excellent cook.
  _____

6 Complete the sentences below. Use a different adverb for each sentence.

~~dangerous~~   easy   fast   hard   loud
patient   quiet   slow

1 Paulo crashed his bike because he rode it
  dangerously .

2 Paulo didn't pass the test because he didn't work _____ .

3 James didn't think that the test was hard. He passed it _____ .

4 Kim was an hour late but Sue waited _____ .

5 Kim plays drums _____ . The neighbours don't like it!

6 Sue practises the piano in the evening. Her little sister is in bed, so she plays _____ .

7 Paulo likes sports. He can run _____ .

8 Sue's father arrived late because he drove _____ .

7 Write sentences about you. Use adverbs and the verbs below.

1 work   2 sing   3 run   4 cook
5 ride   6 speak English

1 _____
2 _____
3 _____
4 _____
5 _____
6 _____

PUZZLE

The mad professor:
– dances excellently.
– eats fast.
– moves noisily.
– rides slowly.
– swims terribly.
How does he play the piano?
1 well   2 quietly   3 badly

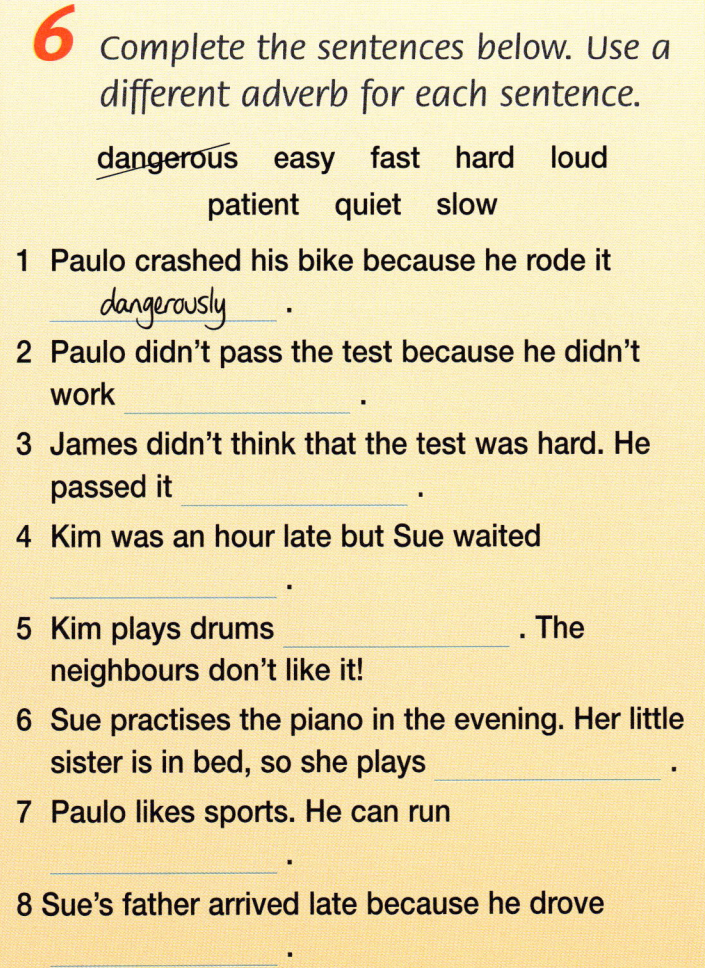

6 Missing meals is bad for you

1a Read the conversation.

KIM: Hi, Paulo. What are you reading?

PAULO: It's about healthy living. Food is important. Eating fruit and vegetables is good for you. Not cooking with oil is a good idea. Missing meals is bad for you. I hate missing meals. Oh, and exercising is important too.

KIM: Healthy living! Yeah, great! Let's go swimming!

PAULO: OK, but I'm hungry – let's have some food first. Burger and chips ...

KIM: Oh, Paulo!

b Are the things below good or bad for you? Write **good** or **bad**.

1 fruit and vegetables _____
2 cooking with oil _____
3 exercising _____

2a Complete the sentences from the text.

1 It's about healthy _____.
2 _____ meals is bad for you.
3 ____ ____ with oil is a good idea.

b Add -ing to the correct verb. Then put the words in the correct order and make sentences.

1 | about | the book | healthy food | eat | is |

2 | healthy food | good for you | is | eat |

3 | bad for you | not | healthy food | is | eat |

3 Write the -ing forms (gerunds) of the verbs below. Put them in the correct sentences.

drive _____   stay _____
go _____   learn _____
lie _____   swim swimming

1 Cats don't like water and hate   swimming .
2 _____ fast is dangerous.
3 Sue's new hobby is _____ the piano.
4 Paulo loves _____ on the beach.
5 _____ up late is bad for you.
6 _____ to bed early is a good idea.

4 Look at the advice about healthy living from Paulo's book. Complete the affirmative and negatives sentences.

Ideas for healthy living:

DON'T	DO
1 cook with oil	5 exercise often
2 smoke	6 eat regularly
3 eat sweets	7 eat fruit and vegetables
4 drink coffee	8 sleep 6–8 hours a night

1   Not cooking   with oil is good.
2 _____ is bad.
3 _____ sweets is good.
4 _____ coffee is good.
5 _____ often is bad.
6 _____ regularly is bad.
7 _____ fruit and vegetables is good.
8 _____ 6–8 hours a night is bad.

CHECK YOUR ANSWERS AND STUDY THE INFORMATION ON PAGE 64.

5a
Read the conversation in exercise 1 again and complete the sentence.

Let's _____ swim _____.

b Now complete the sentences below. Use the correct form of **go** + gerund.

1 Sue _____ swim _____ last week. She swam one kilometre.
2 Sue _____ swim _____. She's doing her homework.
3 _____ Sue _____ swim _____ every week?
4 Sue _____ swim _____ yesterday. She was ill.

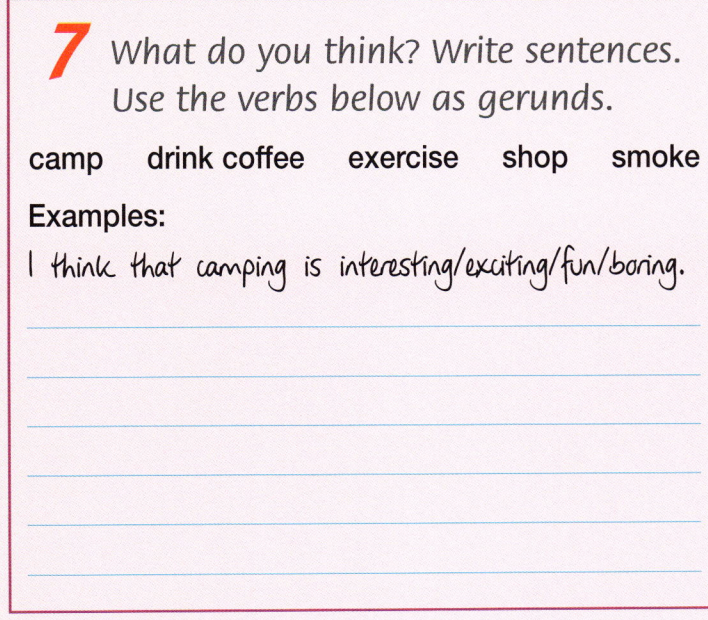

▶▶ CHECK YOUR ANSWERS AND STUDY THE INFORMATION ON PAGE 64.

6
Complete the sentences. Use gerunds of the verbs below with **go** in the correct form.

camp   cycle   jog   shop   ~~swim~~

1 Last summer, I went swimming in the sea every day.
2 I want some new clothes. Let's _____.
3 Let's get healthy! Let's _____.
4 I've got a bike now, so I'm going to _____ at weekends.
5 My aunt loved the countryside and often _____.

7
What do you think? Write sentences. Use the verbs below as gerunds.

camp   drink coffee   exercise   shop   smoke

Examples:
I think that camping is interesting/exciting/fun/boring.
_____
_____
_____
_____
_____

PUZZLE

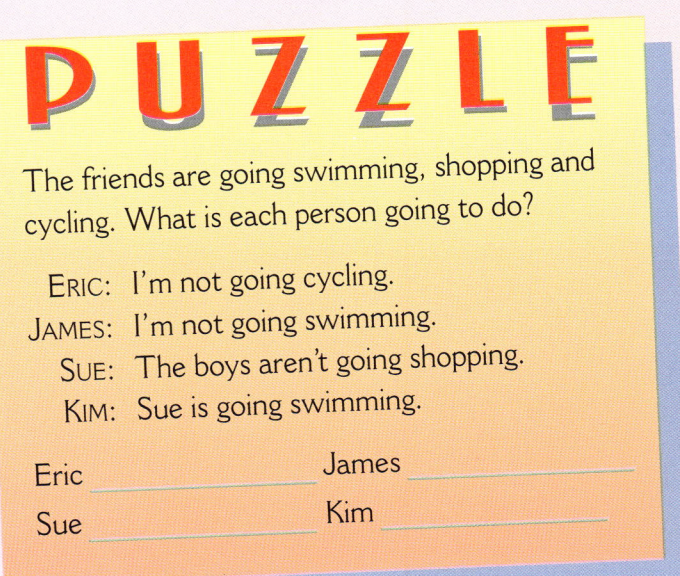

The friends are going swimming, shopping and cycling. What is each person going to do?

ERIC: I'm not going cycling.
JAMES: I'm not going swimming.
SUE: The boys aren't going shopping.
KIM: Sue is going swimming.

Eric _____   James _____
Sue _____   Kim _____

Check point 1-6

1 Lee Murray is in the British band **Let Loose**. Read Lee's answers and write the questions.

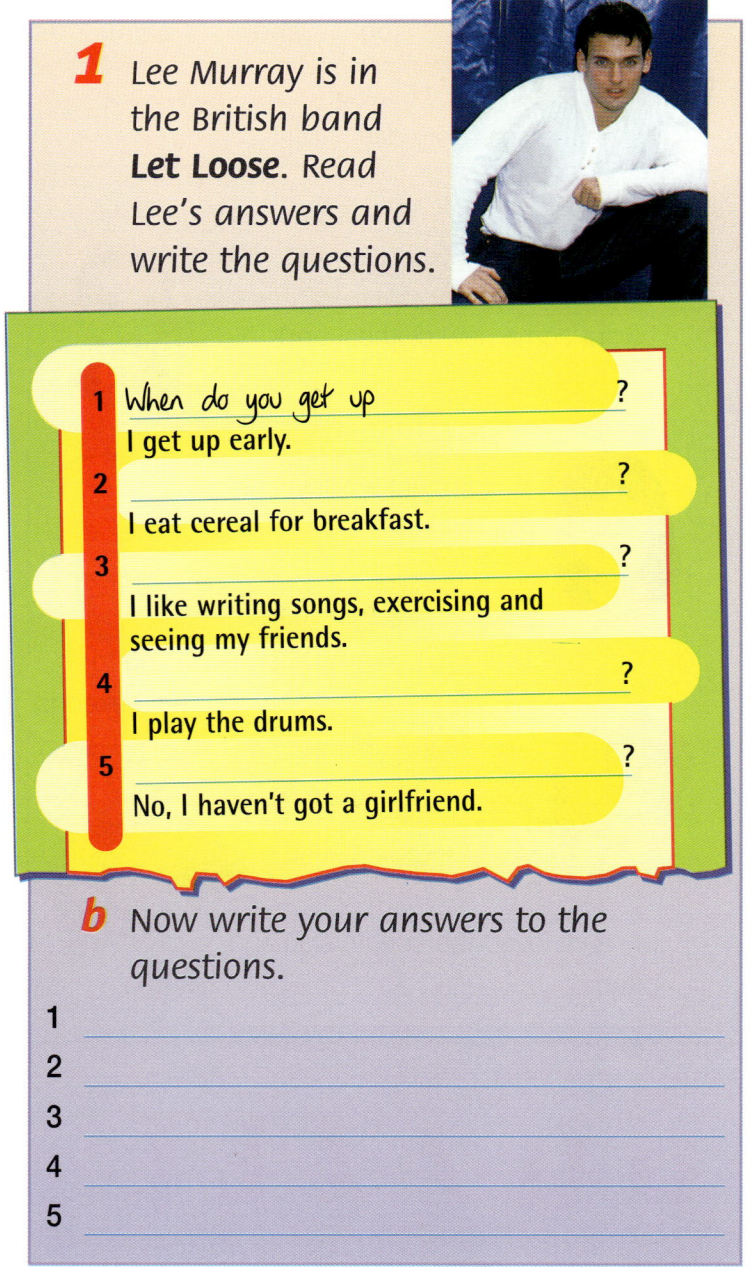

1 When do you get up ?
  I get up early.
2 _____ ?
  I eat cereal for breakfast.
3 _____ ?
  I like writing songs, exercising and seeing my friends.
4 _____ ?
  I play the drums.
5 _____ ?
  No, I haven't got a girlfriend.

b Now write your answers to the questions.

1 _____
2 _____
3 _____
4 _____
5 _____

2 Look at the picture. Complete the sentences below with the correct form of the present simple or continuous.

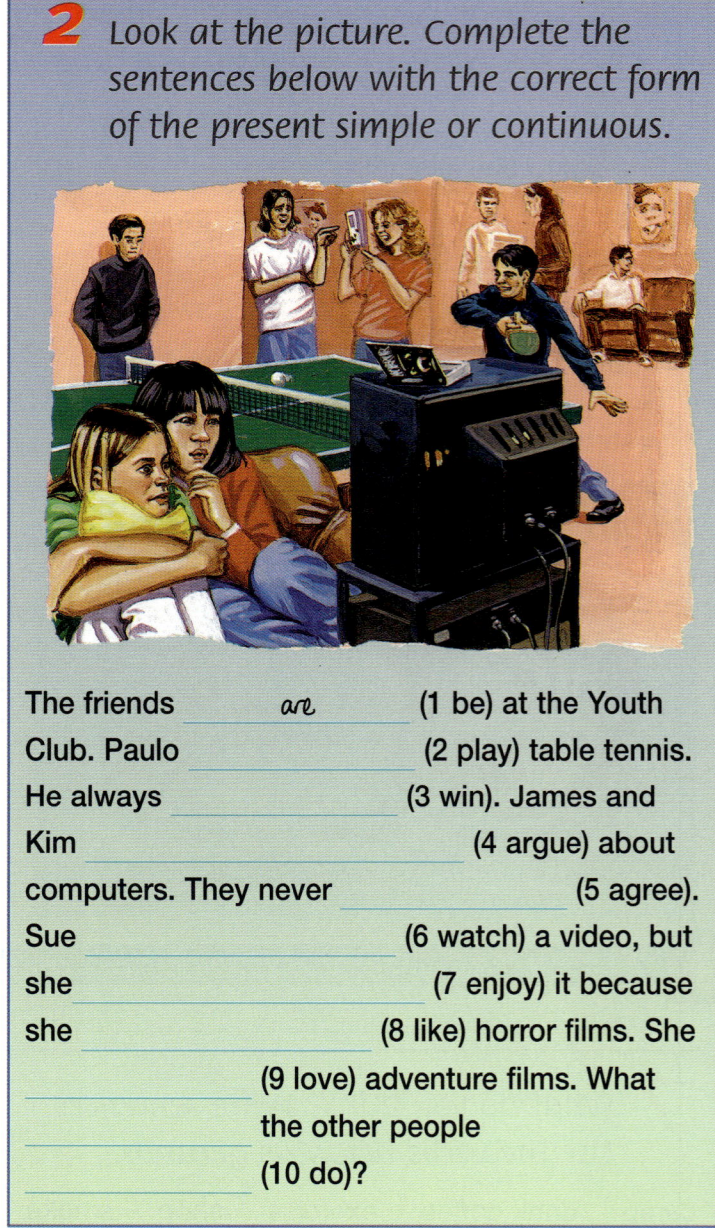

The friends ___are___ (1 be) at the Youth Club. Paulo _____ (2 play) table tennis. He always _____ (3 win). James and Kim _____ (4 argue) about computers. They never _____ (5 agree). Sue _____ (6 watch) a video, but she _____ (7 enjoy) it because she _____ (8 like) horror films. She _____ (9 love) adventure films. What _____ the other people _____ (10 do)?

3 Write sentences about the pictures. Use **going to** + verb and the present continuous with **so** or **because**.

1 It's raining (rain), so she's going to wear (wear) her hat.
2 _____ (study) French _____ (go) to France on holiday.
3 _____ (go) to a café _____ (have) lunch.
4 _____ (snow), _____ (stay) at home.

4a
Look at the map of Alexander the Great's journey. Complete the questions about Alexander. Use the question words below.

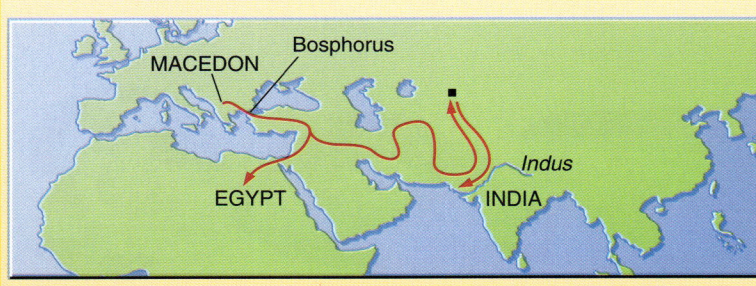

When Where Who ~~Who~~

1 Who   was   his father?
2 _____ _____ he live?
3 _____ _____ his teacher?
4 _____ _____ he go?

b
Now complete the text with the verbs below. Use the past form.

~~be~~ die go go have live stop teach visit

Alexander _was_ (1) the son of <u>King Philip of Macedon</u> (now in Greece). He _____ (2) from 365 to 323 BC. Aristotle _____ (3) him maths, Greek and science. At 22, Alexander and his men _____ (4) to Central Asia. He _____ (5) India but he _____ (6) to China. He _____ (7) at Tashkent. Alexander _____ (8) a long life. He _____ (9) at 32!

c
Now <u>underline</u> the answers to the questions.

5
Put the words below in the correct place. Write a word with the opposite meaning and complete the chart.

~~dangerous~~ good slow quietly

Adjectives		Adverbs	
dangerous	careful	dangerously	

6
Complete the sentences below with words from the chart in exercise 5. Then rewrite each sentence with a gerund.

1 He drives _dangerously_ .
  His driving is dangerous .
2 She cooks _____ .
  _____ .
3 She sings _____ .
  _____ .
4 He reads _____ .
  _____ .

7 Will you go to Mars?

1a Read the magazine text.

Our future in space

There is a robot on Mars now. Its name is Sojourner. We sent it to Mars in 1997. But scientists think that in the future, people will visit Mars. They will find Sojourner, and bring it home. And spaceships will travel to other planets too.

People will live in space stations, and perhaps they'll build cities on the Moon. There isn't any air on the Moon, so people won't live outside, and plants won't grow outside. And there isn't any water, so they'll take it with them from Earth.

When will these things happen? Will we see them? Will you go to Mars?

b Are these pictures of the future? Write **yes** or **no**.

1 _____   2 _____   3 _____

2a Complete the sentences from the text.

+ They _____ cities on the Moon.
− People _____ outside.
? _____ you _____ to Mars?
_____ these things happen?

b Now put the words in the correct order and make sentences.

+ | travel to | People | Mars | will |

− | on the Moon | find | They | won't | water |

? | live | we | Will | in space? |

| will | What | do? | they |

3 Complete the ideas about life in the year 2025. Write affirmative sentences with **will** and the verbs below.

be   do   fly   have   ~~live~~   visit

1 10,000,000,000 people _will live_ on Earth.
2 There _____ cities under the sea.
3 Children _____ spaceships.
4 People _____ Saturn.
5 Robots _____ our difficult work.
6 Children _____ robots for pets.

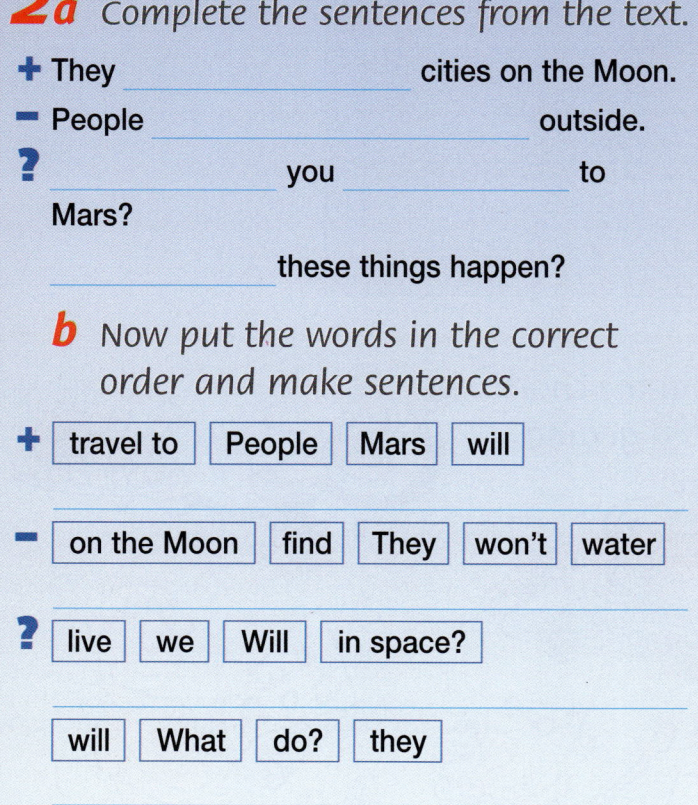

CHECK YOUR ANSWERS AND STUDY THE INFORMATION ON PAGE 64.

4a Now complete these ideas about life in 2025. Write negative sentences with **will** and the verbs below.

be   die   go   grow   live   rain

1 Children _____won't go_____ to school.
2 People _____ on Earth.
3 It _____, so there
4 _____ any water on the Earth.
5 People _____ old.
6 They _____.

b Do you agree with the ideas in exercises 3 and 4?

5 Write questions for these answers about the future. Use the question words below.

How   What   When   Where   Who   Why

1 _Where will we live?_
We'll live on the Moon.
2 _____
We'll live inside because we can't live outside on the Moon.
3 _____
We'll travel by spaceship.
4 _____
Astronauts will build space stations.
5 _____
We'll find the robot, Sojourner, on Mars.
6 _____
It will happen in the future.

6 A boy is asking about his future. Complete the questions and answers. Use the verbs below.

be   do   go   go   have   have
live   travel   visit

– _Will_ I _visit_ (1) other countries?
– No, _____ (2).
– Oh. What _____ I _____ (3)?
– You _____ (4) an astronaut.
You _____ (5) to other planets.
– _____ I _____ (6) to the Moon?
– No, _____ (7). You _____ (8) to Mars!
– Great! _____ I _____ (9) a long life?
– Yes, _____ (10). You _____ (11) to 100 – and you _____ (12) eleven children!
– No, _____ (13)!

7 Write sentences about your future.

_____
_____
_____
_____
_____
_____

PUZZLE
On Ali's 13th birthday, Bob will be 17.
On Bob's 21st birthday, Celia will be 19.
How old will Celia be on Ali's 21st birthday?

8 We shouldn't waste energy

1a Read the text.

b Are these ideas good or bad?

1 We shouldn't walk or cycle. _____
2 We shouldn't travel by car on short journeys. _____
3 We should take baths, not showers. _____
4 We should turn off lights. _____

Should we save energy?

Most countries use coal, oil and gas to make energy.

In some countries, people use wood to heat their homes.

All these forms of energy cause pollution. What should we do?

★ We shouldn't waste energy.
★ We should turn off lights to save electricity.
★ We shouldn't travel by car on short journeys. We should walk or cycle.
★ We should take showers, not baths.

2a Match the sentence parts below.

People use wood • • to save hot water.
People save energy • • to heat their homes.
Some people take showers • • to stop pollution.

b Now complete the sentence with **make**, **use** and **to**.

Some countries _____ the wind _____ energy.

 CHECK YOUR ANSWERS AND STUDY THE INFORMATION ON PAGE 65.

3 Complete the sentences. Use the correct form of a verb from list A with a verb from list B to complete the sentences.

A
buy   get up   ride   stay up   use   visit

B
go   make   read   save   take   watch

1 Most countries __use__ coal __to make__ energy.
2 Yesterday she _____ late _____ a nature programme on TV.
3 He _____ early tomorrow _____ jogging.
4 He _____ his grandma every day _____ her dog for a walk.
5 She always _____ her bike to school _____ energy.
6 Let's _____ a book _____ about pollution.

4a Complete the sentences from the text in exercise 1.

+ We _____ take showers.
− We _____ travel by car.
? _____ we save energy?
  What _____ we do?

b Now put the words in the correct order and make sentences.

+ | I | energy | save | should |

_____

− | energy | waste | shouldn't | they |

_____

? | we | baths | should | take |

_____ ?

| should | we | how | travel |

_____ ?

➤➤➤ CHECK YOUR ANSWERS AND STUDY THE INFORMATION ON PAGE 65.

5 Write sentences about the pictures. Use **should/shouldn't** and the verbs below.

bite close drive drop play turn off

1 He **should close** the door.

2 She _____ the tap.

3 They _____ litter.

4 She _____ fast.

5 They _____ with matches.

6 He _____ his fingernails.

6 Complete the text. Use **should/shouldn't** and the verbs below.

close do help keep recycle save
~~think~~ turn off use waste

We **should think** (1) about the future.
What _____ we _____ (2)
_____ (3) our planet?
We _____ (4) energy.
We _____ (5) lights.
We _____ (6) doors
_____ (7) heat in.
We _____ (8) glass bottles again.
And we _____ (9) paper
_____ (10) trees.

7 Think of three different things we **should/shouldn't** do to help our planet.

_____
_____
_____

PUZZLE

A farmer is going to cross a river. He's got his dog, his goat and a big bag of apples. His boat is very small, so he can only take one thing with him. He shouldn't leave the goat with the apples – the goat will eat the apples! He shouldn't leave the dog with the goat – the dog will bite the goat! What should he do?

9 Are you doing anything next Saturday?

1a Eric is telephoning his friend Liam. Read their conversation.

ERIC: Hello, Liam.
LIAM: Hi, Eric.
ERIC: My parents are going away next weekend. They're visiting somebody.
LIAM: Why are you speaking quietly?
ERIC: Because I'm going to have a party – but I can't ask them. They'll say no.
LIAM: A secret party. They'll be angry.
ERIC: They won't know – nothing will go wrong! Are you doing anything next Saturday?
LIAM: Oh, sorry. Yes, I am. I'm going somewhere with my parents. I'm not doing anything on Sunday. How about Sunday?
ERIC: Yeah, OK. I'll tell Kim and Sue and ... everybody!
LIAM: OK. I'll see you on Sunday.

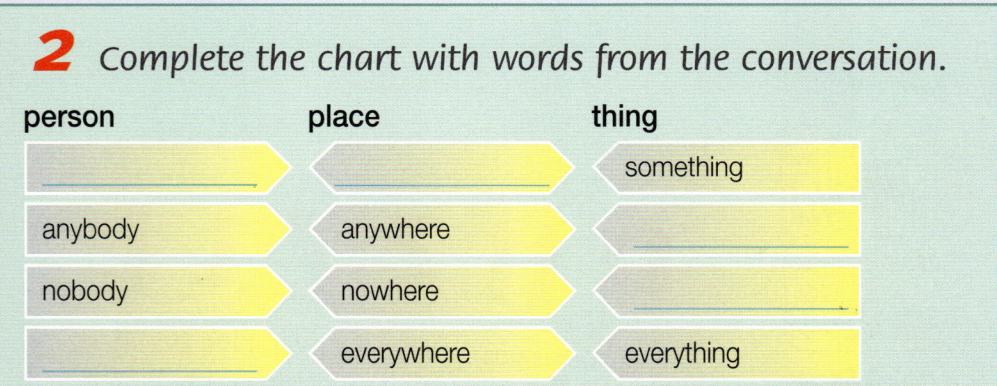

b Look at these sentences from the conversation. Are they talking about the present or the future?

1 They're visiting somebody. _____   2 I'm going somewhere. _____

2 Complete the chart with words from the conversation.

person	place	thing
_____	_____	something
anybody	anywhere	_____
nobody	nowhere	_____
_____	everywhere	everything

3a Complete the sentences from the conversation.

+ They're visiting _____ body.
  I'm going _____ where.
− I'm not doing _____ thing.
? Are you doing _____ thing?

b Now complete the sentences below.

+ She's doing _____.
− We're not meeting _____.
  He's not going _____.
? Is he going _____?
  Are you meeting _____?

 CHECK YOUR ANSWERS AND STUDY THE INFORMATION ON PAGE 66.

4 Complete the sentences with different indefinite pronouns.

1 Listen! There's ___someone___ at the door.
2 He always stays at home. He never goes _____ .
3 I can't see. There's _____ in my eye.
4 Please find it! Look _____ !
5 His homework was terrible. _____ was wrong.
6 Yesterday was very boring. _____ happened.
7 Where are you going? _____ ! I'm staying here.

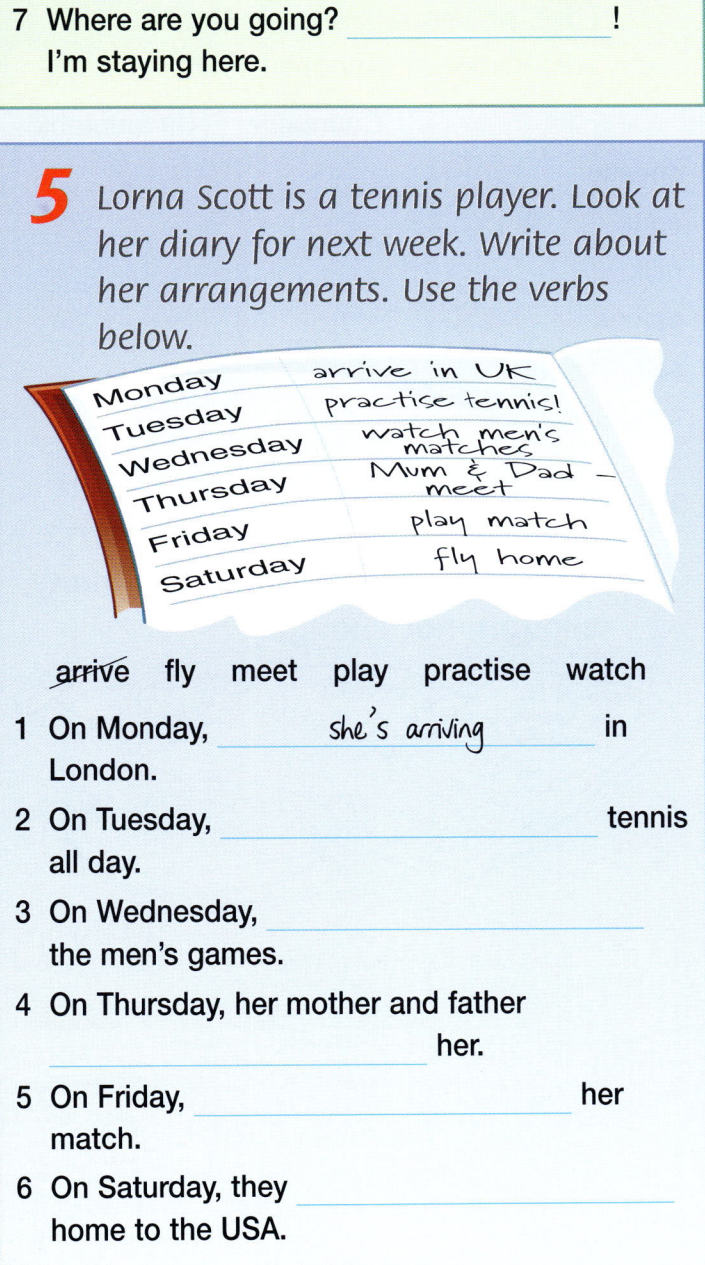

5 Lorna Scott is a tennis player. Look at her diary for next week. Write about her arrangements. Use the verbs below.

Monday	arrive in UK
Tuesday	practise tennis!
Wednesday	watch men's matches
Thursday	Mum & Dad – meet
Friday	play match
Saturday	fly home

~~arrive~~   fly   meet   play   practise   watch

1 On Monday, ___she's arriving___ in London.
2 On Tuesday, _____ tennis all day.
3 On Wednesday, _____ the men's games.
4 On Thursday, her mother and father _____ her.
5 On Friday, _____ her match.
6 On Saturday, they _____ home to the USA.

6 Lorna is talking to a sports writer about next week. Use the words below and indefinite pronouns to complete their conversation.

1 you / do / INDEFINITE PRONOUN / next week?
   ___Are you doing anything next week?___
2 Yes, I / go / London.
   _____
3 you / play / tennis with / INDEFINITE PRONOUN?
   _____
4 I / play / Friday with / INDEFINITE PRONOUN.
   _____
5 you / go / INDEFINITE PRONOUN / after London?
   _____
6 No, I / come / home / USA.
   _____

7 Write sentences about your arrangements for the future.

Example: ___I'm meeting my friend tonight.___

PUZZLE

There are two computers ZX1 and ZX2. ZX1 always gives correct information; everything is true. ZX2 is broken, and always gives false information; nothing is true. But which computer is ZX1? You don't know, so you can't believe anything! You can ask one computer one question to find ZX1. Write your question.

23

10 There aren't enough girls

1a Eric is having his party. Read the conversations.

- I'm hungry. Is there any food?
- Yes, there is. It's on the table. I think that there's enough.
- There's enough salad but there are only seven sandwiches.
- Most people at this party are boys. There are too many boys. There aren't enough girls.
- I don't like this drink. It's too sweet. There's too much sugar.
- I'm going to turn up the music. I can't hear it. It's not loud enough.
- No! The neighbours will hear!

b Answer the questions with **yes** or **no**.

1 Are there any sandwiches? _____
2 Is Sue's drink sweet? _____
3 Does Kim think that the music is loud? _____

c Look at the recipe for the drink at Eric's party. Match the words with the pictures.

enough •
too much •
not enough •

2a Complete the sentences from the text with **too** or **enough**.

1 There _____ salad.
2 There _____ girls.
3 There _____ sugar.
4 There _____ boys.

b Now complete these <u>false</u> sentences about the party.

1 There _____ too _____ sandwiches.
2 There _____ not _____ boys.
3 There _____ too _____ girls.
4 There _____ not _____ sugar.

CHECK YOUR ANSWERS AND STUDY THE INFORMATION ON PAGE 66.

3a Look at the nouns. Are they countable or uncountable?

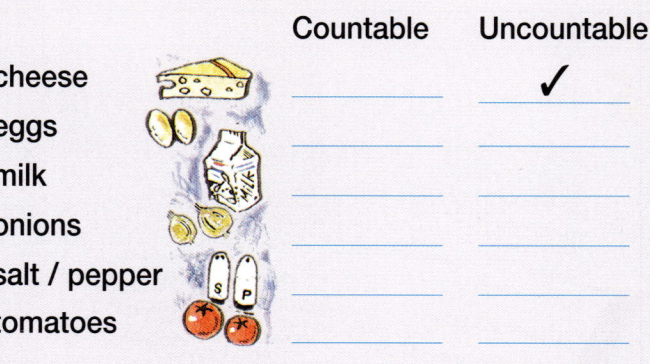

	Countable	Uncountable
cheese		✓
eggs		
milk		
onions		
salt / pepper		
tomatoes		

b Look at the recipe. Now look at the pictures of food for the recipe. Write sentences. Use **too much**, **too many**, **enough**, **not enough**.

1 There are too many eggs.
2 _____
3 _____
4 _____
5 _____

4a Put the words in the correct order to make sentences from the conversation in exercise 1.

1 `sweet` `too` `It's`
   _____

2 `not` `enough` `loud` `It's`
   _____

b Now put these words in the correct order and make sentences. Match them with the pictures.

1 hot isn't It enough
   _____

2 hot It's too
   _____

3 enough hot It's
   _____

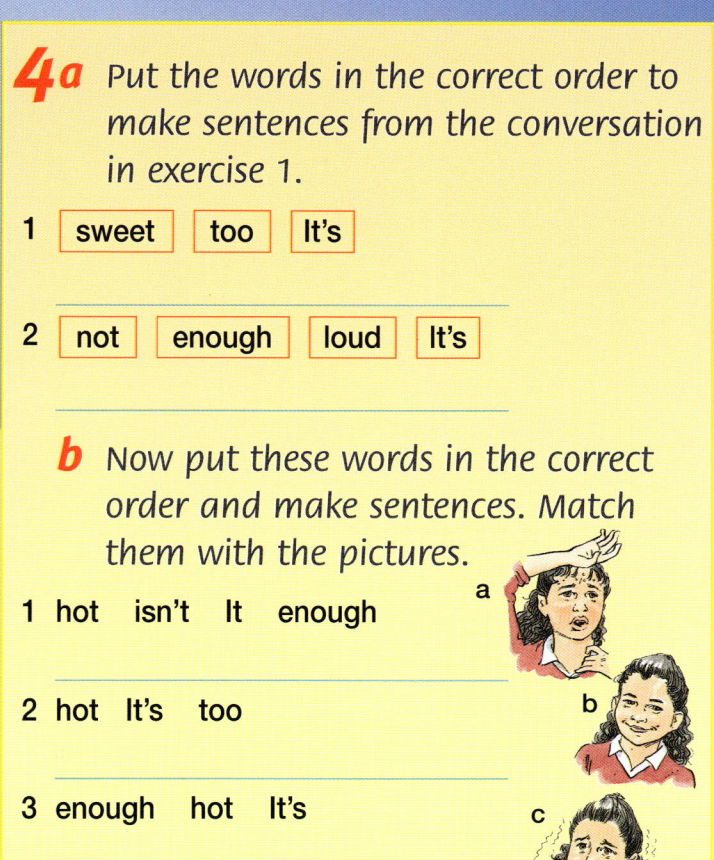

 CHECK YOUR ANSWERS AND STUDY THE INFORMATION ON PAGE 66.

5 Write sentences. Use **too**, **enough**, **not enough**.

1 This coffee is fine.
   It's sweet enough.   (sweet)
2 I can't do my homework.
   _____ (difficult)
3 Paulo's little brother can't drive a car.
   He _____ (old)
4 This jumper is the right size.
   It _____ (big)
5 The dog can't catch the rabbit.
   The rabbit _____
   (fast)
6 Kim can't find her book.
   _____ (tidy)
7 He hates playing basketball.
   _____ (tall)

6 Complete the sentences. Use the adjectives below.

heavy hot serious sunny sweet

1 *There's too much* sugar.
   It's too sweet .
2 _____
   cold water in the bath.
   _____ .
3 _____
   pictures in the book.
   _____ .
4 _____
   rainy days in Britain.
   _____ .
5 _____
   water in the buckets.
   _____ .

7 Write about your town. Use **too**, **enough**, **not enough**. Use the words below to help.

big busy cinemas exciting shops

_____
_____
_____
_____

PUZZLE

Find food and drink words in the square.

```
M F R U I T E S
I C E C H R E A M
L A C O I E L E
K K O D P L G A
K E D I S L G T
C R I L A P S Y
S A L   D   T A
```

How many words have you got? Have you got enough? You should have 12.

11 The biggest in the world!

1a Read the student's notes about dinosaurs.

b Match the names with the pictures.

1 The Ultrasaurus • • a
2 The Brachiosaurus • • b
3 The Mamenchisaurus • • c

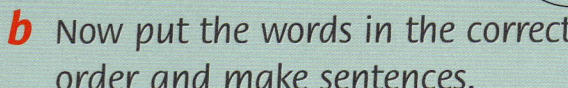

Dinosaurs lived from 210 million to 65 million years ago.

1 The Ultrasaurus was <u>the tallest dinosaur</u>. It was 18 m tall.

2 The Brachiosaurus was <u>heavier than</u> the Ultrasaurus. The Brachiosaurus was the heaviest dinosaur and weighed 78 tonnes. It was as heavy as 13 elephants.

3 The Mamenchisaurus had <u>the longest neck</u>. It was 10 m long.

4 The Tyrannosaurus wasn't as tall as the Ultrasaurus, but it had <u>the biggest teeth</u>. They were 15 cm and very sharp.

2a Read the sentences below and write A, B and C on the circles.

A is larger than B.
B is not as large as C.
C is as large as A.

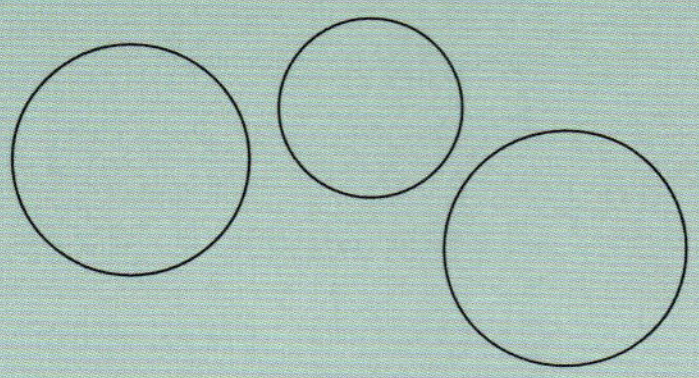

b Now put the words in the correct order and make sentences.

1 | B | is | C | than | smaller |

2 | as | B | isn't | A | small | as |

c Match the correct endings with the adjectives.

big • • -er / -est
large • • -ger / -gest
long • • -ier / -iest
heavy • • -r / -st
tall • • -er / -est

What are the spelling rules?

3 Complete the chart below.

adjective	comparative	superlative
		the cheapest
fast		
		the friendliest
hot		
		the nicest
small		

 CHECK YOUR ANSWERS AND STUDY THE INFORMATION ON PAGE 67.

4 Use the words below and write sentences with comparatives.

1 A whale _is bigger than a monkey._ (big/monkey)
2 An elephant _is not as tall as a giraffe._ (tall/giraffe)
3 A tortoise _____ (slow/cat)
4 A cat _____ (fast/cheetah)
5 A dog _____ (friendly/lion)
6 A mouse _____ (small/tortoise)
7 A monkey _____ (strong/elephant)

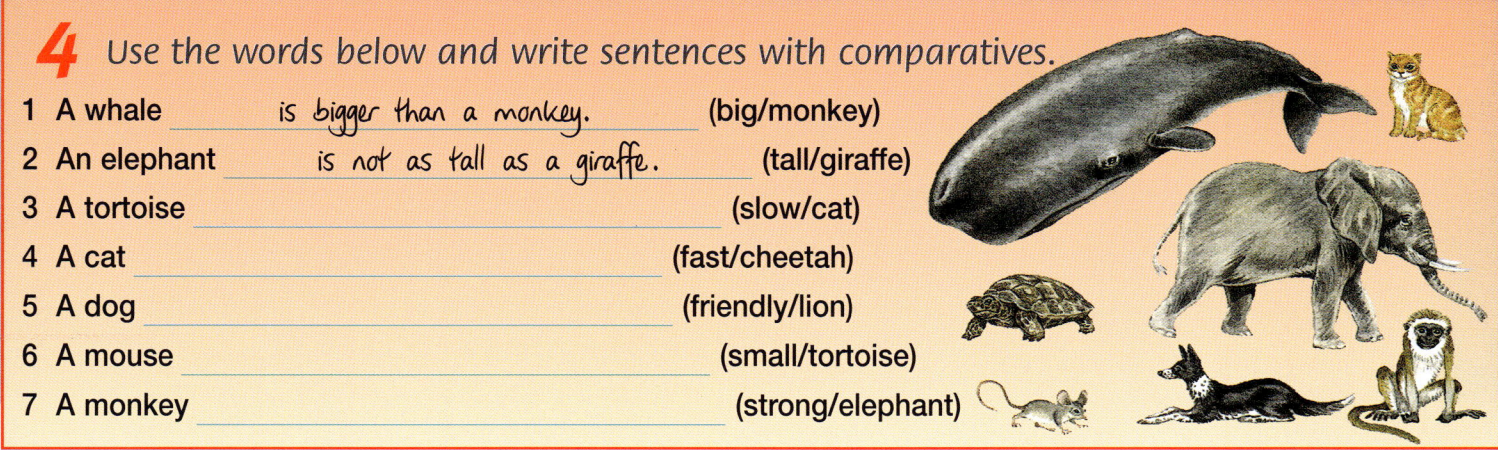

5 Complete these sentences from a book about dinosaurs.

The large dinosaurs _were_ (1) large r (2) _than_ (3) elephants and tall ___ (4) ___ (5) giraffes. The Compsognathus ___ (6) ___ (7) small ___ (8) dinosaur. It ___ (9) ___ (10) small ___ (11) a cat. The Brachiosaurus ___ (12) ___ (13) big ___ (14) dinosaur but it ___ (15) ___ (16) big ___ (17) the Blue Whale. The Blue Whale ___ (18) ___ (19) large ___ (20) animal in the world today.

6 Look at the information below and write sentences about the UK.

The top ten in the UK	big cities	long rivers	tall buildings	old universities	rich people
1	London 7 million	The Severn 354 km	Canary Wharf 244 m	Oxford 1249	Elizabeth II £100 million

1 _London is the biggest city._
2 _____
3 _____
4 _____
5 _____

7 Now write about your country.

1 _____ is the biggest city.
2 _____
3 _____
4 _____
5 _____

PUZZLE

Before Cook found Australia, what was the biggest island in the world?

12 It's the best!

1a Kim and her parents are going to go on holiday to Scotland. Kim is reading the tourist brochure.

Come to Scotland
Visit great forests and quiet villages, see exciting towns, castles, beautiful gardens, interesting shops and museums.

Come to Kelso in The Borders
Sir Walter Scott said Kelso was:

'The most beautiful and romantic town in Scotland'.

Our top two hotels in Kelso:

Black Swan Hotel

This is a family hotel – smaller and friendlier than most hotels in town – in the centre of Kelso. Excellent home cooking.

Bedrooms: 3 Bathrooms: 3
Price per person: £19 – £35

Sunlaws House Hotel

Sunlaws is further from the city centre than the Black Swan Hotel, quieter and more peaceful. It is also more expensive than the Black Swan. In fact, it is the most expensive hotel in Kelso – but many people say it's the best!

Bedrooms: 22
Bathrooms: 22
Price per person: £94.50

b How many stars do you think the tourist brochure gives each hotel?
(* = good, ***** = excellent)

Black Swan _____   Sunlaws House _____

2a How many syllables are there in the words below?

beautiful	3	exciting	___
expensive	___	far	___
friendly	___	interesting	___
peaceful	___	quiet	___
romantic	___	small	___

b Six adjectives in the list above use **more** and **most**. Underline the words.

c What is the rule?

 CHECK YOUR ANSWERS AND STUDY THE INFORMATION ON PAGE 67.

3 Complete the chart below.

adjective	comparative	superlative
boring		
exciting		
		furthest
	friendlier	
		the best
intelligent		
polite		
quiet		
	more serious	
	worse	

4 Kim is phoning hotels in Kelso. She wants to find a cheaper hotel. Look at her notes. What does she say to her parents? Complete her sentences with comparatives and superlatives of the words below.

1 cheap   2 cheap   3 peaceful   4 far
5 interesting   6 good

Ivy House, £60, 5km → town centre, very quiet.
Fernlands £80, town centre, Motor Museum (ghost)
The Bell, £100, town centre.

Fernlands is great! It's ___cheaper than___ (1) The Bell but it's _____ (2) Ivy House. I know that you want a quiet holiday. Ivy House _____ (3), and it's _____ (4) from town. But Fernlands is _____ (5) than Ivy House. It's next to the Motor Museum, and it's got a ghost! It's _____ (6)!

6 What do you think? Write sentences. Use **more ... / -er than**, **not as ... as**, **as ... as**.

1 _____
Ford/Porsche – beautiful
2 _____
orange juice/coffee – healthy
3 _____
computers/museums – interesting
4 _____
boys/girls – intelligent
5 _____
English/maths – difficult

5 Look at the photos of two cars in the Motor Museum. Write sentences and use **more ... / ... -er than** or **not as ... as**.

1 The Ford ___is older than the Porsche.___ (old)
2 The Porsche _____ (exciting)
3 The Ford _____ (comfortable)
4 The Porsche _____ (fast)
5 The Porsche _____ (long)

7 Describe your family. Use the words below.

happy   intelligent   interesting
quiet   serious   young

1 _____ is the happiest person.
2 _____
3 _____
4 _____
5 _____
6 _____
7 _____

PUZZLE

Don't use a ruler. Tick the longest line.

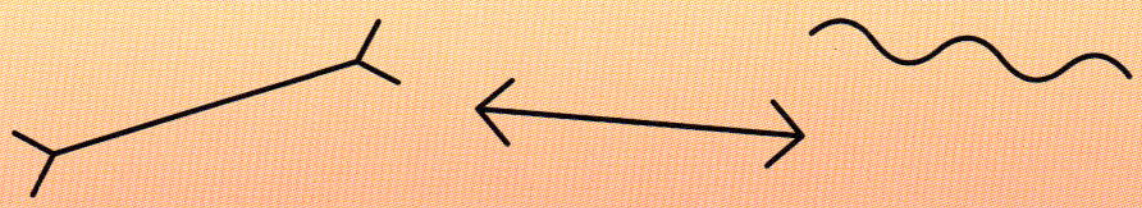

Check point 7–12

1 It's the morning after Eric's party. Eric's parents are coming home in the evening. What will happen? Use the verbs below. Write sentences with **will/won't**.

be   find   ~~see~~   shout   talk to   turn on

1 They _will see_ the dirty glasses everywhere.
2 The video _____.
3 They _____ the broken bowl.
4 The neighbours _____ his parents about the noisy party.
5 His parents _____ happy.
6 Eric's father _____ at him!

2 What should Eric do? Match the sets of words. Then write sentences with **should**.

1 pick up / litter   •   • buy / new bowl
2 take / glasses to
   the kitchen   •   • ask about / video
3 telephone /
   video shop   •   • tidy / room
4 go / shop   •   • give them / present
5 visit / neighbours   •   • wash them

1 _He should pick up the litter to tidy the room._
2 _____
3 _____
4 _____
5 _____

3 Complete the conversations. Use the present continuous and the words below.

~~anything~~   anything   everywhere   nobody   something   somewhere

Are you _doing_ (1 do) _anything_ (2) this afternoon? My parents _____ (3 come) home this evening and _____ (4) is untidy.

I _____ (5 do) _____ (6) at 2.

What _____ you _____ (7 do)?

I _____ (8 have) a piano lesson.

Liam, please help! The house is untidy. Sue _____ (9 go) _____ (10). I telephoned Kim's house, but _____ (11) was at home. My parents _____ (12 arrive) at about 6.

I _____ (13 do) _____ (14). I'll see you in 20 minutes.

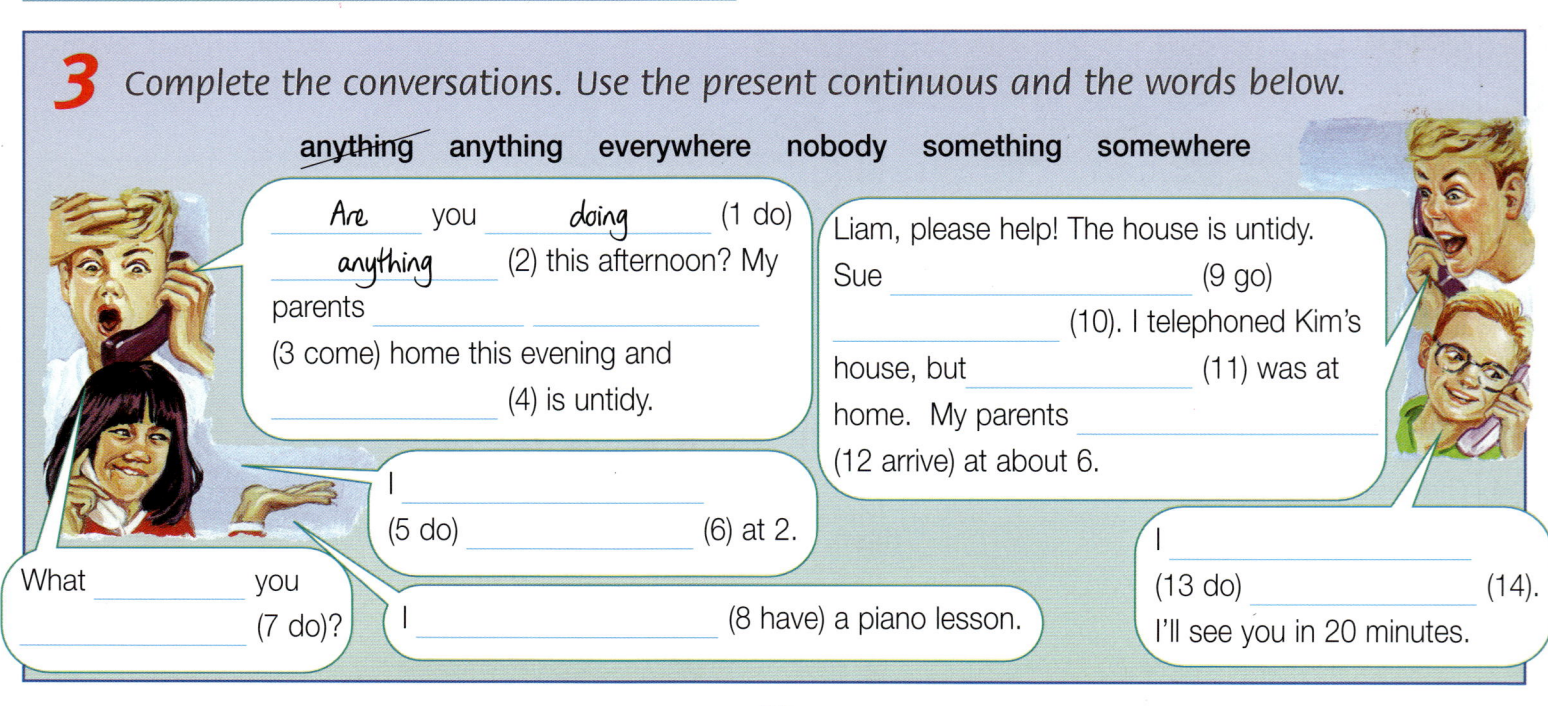

4 Look at the pictures and complete the sentences. Use the adjectives below.

difficult   healthy   heavy   strong   ~~sunny~~

1 _There are too many_ clouds. _It's not sunny enough._
2 _____ milk in this coffee. _____
3 _____ oil in my food. _____
4 _____ questions in my homework. _____
5 _____ people to move the piano. _____

5 Complete the sentences. Compare the Compsognathus and the Tyrannosaurus Rex.

1 The Compsognathus _was not as strong as_ (strong) the T Rex.
2 The T Rex _____ (frightening) the Compsognathus.
3 The Compsognathus _____ (dangerous) the T Rex.
4 The Compsognathus _____ (small) the T Rex.
5 The Compsognathus _____ (heavy) the T Rex.
6 The T Rex _____ (noisy) the Compsognathus.

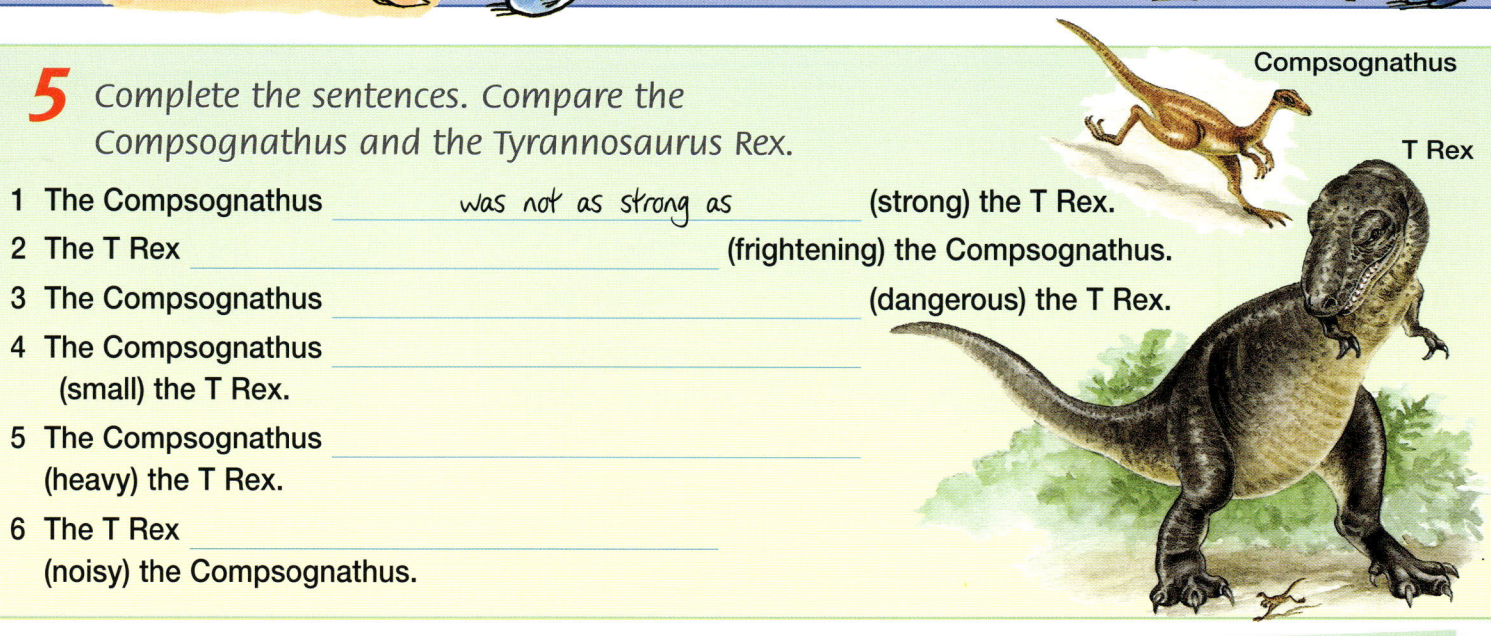

6 Look at the information below. Complete the sentences with the correct form of **long** and **high**.

1 The Nile _is the longest_ river in the world.
2 The Amazon _____ the Yangtse.
3 The Amazon _____ the Nile.
4 K2 _____ Kanchenjunga.
5 Kanchenjunga _____ K2.
6 Everest _____ mountain in the world.

Rivers in the World — km
1 The Nile, Africa — 6,695
2 The Amazon, S America — 6,570
3 The Yangtse, Asia — 6,380

Mountains in the World — m
1 Everest, Nepal — 8,848
2 K2, Kashmir/Sinkiang — 8,611
3 Kanchenjunga, Nepal/Sikkim — 8,586

13 It was rising from the sea

1a Read the text.

b Answer the questions.

1. Is the text talking about the past, present or future? _____
2. Did the fishermen see a boat? _____
3. What did they see? _____

One afternoon, in 1963, some fishermen were fishing in the Atlantic Ocean near Iceland. While they were fishing, they saw something in the distance. It was on fire and they thought that it was another boat. They were sailing nearer when it suddenly grew larger. They weren't looking at a boat, they were looking at a new island. It was rising from the sea. It grew to 200 m high in only ten days. Now its name is Surtsey Island and it is 1.9 km².

2a Complete the sentences from the text.

past continuous
+ They _____ look _____ at a new island.
− They _____ look _____ at a boat.

when/while
_____ they were fishing _____ they saw something. They were sailing nearer _____ it suddenly grew larger.

b Now complete these sentences.

past continuous
+ They _____ sail _____ in the Atlantic.
− The island _____ grow _____ smaller.

when/while
They were fishing _____ they saw something. _____ they were sailing nearer _____ it grew larger.

➤➤➤ CHECK YOUR ANSWERS ON PAGE 68 AND STUDY THE INFORMATION.

3 Last Saturday, Ann, Bill and Colin were visiting Scotland. Look at the picture and complete the sentences. Use the past continuous and the verbs below.

drink   eat   ~~fish~~   rise   sit down   stand up

1. They _____were fishing._____
2. Ann _____ a sandwich.
3. Bill and Colin _____ some tea.
4. Colin _____
5. Ann and Bill _____
6. A monster _____ from the water!

4 Now read the newspaper report. <u>Underline</u> five false things in the report. Write true sentences to correct the information.

1 They weren't walking. They were fishing.
2 Ann _____
_____
3 Bill and Colin _____
_____
4 It _____
5 It _____

Holiday horror!

Ann, Bill and Colin <u>were walking</u> in Scotland last Saturday, when something strange happened. At about 2 o'clock, Ann was taking photos. Bill and Colin were collecting stones when suddenly a monster appeared. It was running from the forest and looking at them angrily.

5 Match the sentence parts.

1 Kim was playing with her sister's baby •
2 While Sue was playing with her rabbit, •
3 While the friends were fishing, •
4 The friends were fishing •
5 While James was cycling home, •

• it started to rain.
• when it started to rain.
• it bit her.
• his bike broke.
• when it bit her.

6 Complete the sentences about the pictures. Use the past continuous, the past simple, **when** or **while** and the verbs below.

arrive break come eat meet sing walk write

1 She _was walking_ to school _when_ she _____ a friend.
2 The dog _____ his lunch _____ he _____ into his room.
3 _____ they _____ on the board, the teacher _____ . 
4 _____ she _____ , _____ the window _____ .

7 Complete the sentences about you.

1 I was _____
at 6.15 yesterday morning.
2 _____
at 2 pm last Saturday.
3 _____
at 8.15 this morning.
4 _____
at 7.45 yesterday evening.
5 _____
at 10 am last Sunday.

PUZZLE

Read and do the puzzle from many years ago.

When I was going to St Ives,
I met a man with seven wives.
Each wife had seven sacks,
Each sack had seven *kits.
Kits, cats, sacks, wives,
How many were going to St Ives? _____

(*kit = old word for kitten, baby cat)

14 Which one was driving?

1a Read Sue's conversation with the police officer.

Where were you standing?   Next to the telephones.
Which ones?   The new ones in front of the newsagent's.
What happened?   The bus was driving away from the traffic lights when a car crossed the road and hit the bus.
Who was driving the car?   The short man. The one in the red jumper.
Was he driving fast?   Yes, he was.
What happened next?   All the men got out and started shouting. They were arguing when one man hit the bus driver.
Which one hit the bus driver?   The one with the black eye!

b Are these sentences true (T) or false (F)?

1 Sue was in the newsagent's. _____   2 The driver's jumper was red. _____

2a Complete the sentences below from the conversation. Then match the questions with the answers.

1 _____ _____ you stand _____ ? •   • Yes, he was.
2 _____ _____ driv _____ ? •   • The short man.
3 _____ he driv _____ fast? •   • Next to the telephones.

b Now complete the sentences and match the questions with the answers.

1 _____ was stand _____ next to the telephones? •   • The accident.
2 _____ the men speak _____ quietly to the bus driver? •   • Sue.
3 _____ they argu _____ about? •   • No, they weren't.

CHECK YOUR ANSWERS AND STUDY THE INFORMATION ON PAGES 68–69.

3 What was the driver doing before the accident? Look at the pictures and write questions and short answers. Use the verbs below.

~~drive~~   read   talk   wait   watch   wear

1 Was he driving   fast?   Yes, he was.
2 _____   at the lights?   _____
3 _____   the road?   _____
4 _____   a newspaper?   _____
5 _____   to his friends?   _____
6 _____   a seat belt?   _____

4a
Look at the conversation in exercise 1 again and complete the sentences below with **one** or **ones**.

1 He was wearing a jumper.
   It was a red _____ .
2 The phones are new. They're new _____ .
3 Who are these men?
   The _____ in the car.
4 Do you remember this car? 
   It's the _____ in the accident.

b
Now complete the questions and answers with **Which** and **one** or **ones**.

1 _____ car was he driving? The white _____ . 
2 _____ phones are new? The small _____ .

→ CHECK YOUR ANSWERS AND STUDY THE INFORMATION ON PAGE 69.

5
Look at the picture and complete the questions and answers. Use **Which**, the past continuous, **one** or **ones** and the verbs below.

carry   climb   jump   throw

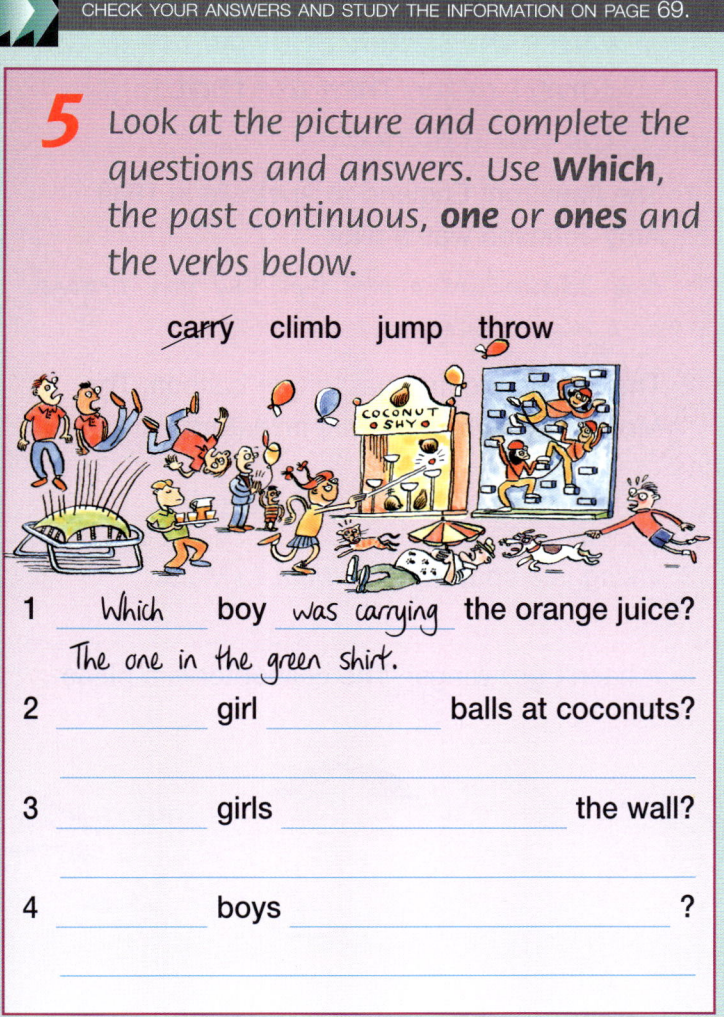

1 Which boy was carrying the orange juice?
  The one in the green shirt.
2 _____ girl _____ balls at coconuts?
3 _____ girls _____ the wall?
4 _____ boys _____ ?

6
Look at the picture in exercise 5 again. Write questions for the answers below. Use the past continuous and the verbs below.

carry   do   lie   ~~sleep~~

1 Who was sleeping?
  The old man.
2 _____ the old man _____
  Under the umbrella.
3 _____ the dog _____
  It was chasing the cat.
4 _____
  the orange juice?
  The boy in the green shirt.

7
Write your answers for the questions below.

1 Where were you and what were you doing at 7.15 yesterday evening?

2 Were you sitting or standing?

3 What were you wearing?

PUZZLE
Look at the footprint and the shoes. Which one was the person wearing?

15 He is the pilot that built the smallest plane

1a Read the information.

b Are the sentences below true (T) or false (F)?

1 The Wright brothers invented the aeroplane. _____
2 *Concorde* is not as fast as *Flyer 1*. _____
3 A pilot built the smallest plane. _____

- Orville and Wilbur Wright were brothers who invented the aeroplane. In 1903, they built an aeroplane which flew 36.5 metres at 48 kilometres an hour. Its name was *Flyer 1*.

Planes today fly faster and further. *Concorde* is a passenger plane that can fly across the Atlantic at 2,300 kilometres an hour. The biggest passenger plane is the 747/400. It can carry 567 people and is 70.7 metres long.

This is Robert H Starr. He is the pilot that built the smallest plane. *Bumble Bee* is only 2.64 metres long but it can fly at 306 kilometres an hour. *Bumble Bee* is smaller than *Flyer 1* but faster!

2a Put the groups of words from the text in the correct order to make sentences.

1 | built the smallest plane | he is the pilot | that |

2 | that | *Concorde* is a passenger plane | can fly at 2,300 kilometres an hour |

b Now put these groups of words in the correct order.

1 | *Bumble Bee* is a plane | is only 2.6 metres long | that |

2 | flew the first plane | that | the Wright brothers were the pilots |

3 Check the sentences below are in the correct order. Then use **that** to join the two sentences.

1 She flew from England to Australia in 1930. Amy Johnson was a pilot.
Amy Johnson was a pilot that flew from England to Australia in 1930.

2 They made the first passenger balloon. The Montgolfier brothers were inventors.
_____

3 *Viking* is a spaceship. It went to Mars.
_____

4 It hasn't got wings! The helicopter is a plane.
_____

CHECK YOUR ANSWERS AND STUDY THE INFORMATION ON PAGE 69.

4a Complete the sentences from the text.
1 Orville and Wilbur Wright were <u>brothers</u> _____ invented the aeroplane
2 They built <u>an aeroplane</u> _____ flew 36.5 metres.

b Use **who** or **which** to complete the sentences below.
1 Robert H Starr is <u>the man</u> _____ flew the smallest plane.
2 *Concorde* is <u>a plane</u> _____ carries passengers.

c Now complete the table with **who**, **which** and **that**.

| that | person | |
| | thing | |

> CHECK YOUR ANSWERS AND STUDY THE INFORMATION ON PAGE 69.

5 Use the correct form of the verbs below and **who** or **which** to complete the sentences.

carry   drive   fly   have got   ~~ride~~   travel

1 <u>A cyclist</u> is a person <u>who rides a bike.</u>
2 _____ is a vehicle _____ two wheels.
3 _____ is a person _____.
4 _____ is a vehicle _____ in the air.
5 _____ is a person _____.
6 _____ is a vehicle _____ passengers.

6 Match the people and things to their definitions. Then write sentences with **who**, **which** or **that** and **someone/something**.

- spaceship
- doctor
- sailor
- camera
- submarine

- helps sick people
- sails ships
- sails under the sea
- travels in space
- takes photographs

1 <u>A spaceship is something which travels in space.</u>
2 _____
3 _____
4 _____
5 _____

7 Write about the people and things below in the same way as exercise 6.

1 friend   2 ship   3 teacher   4 train

1 <u>A friend is someone who</u> _____
2 _____
3 _____
4 _____

PUZZLE

I've got a friend who has got a parrot. The parrot can say every word that it hears. But the parrot never says anything. Why?

16 I really enjoyed myself

1a Read the conversation between Paulo and his friend Elena.

- Did you both enjoy yourselves at the football match?
- Hi, Elena. I really enjoyed myself and I think that Carlos enjoyed himself too.
- Then we went home and we saw ourselves on TV. We were watching the match on video …
- … we were laughing at each other when the video stopped. It ate the tape and turned itself off.
- I thought that your video was broken. Did you telephone the video repair shop?
- No, we repaired it ourselves.

b Are these sentences true (T) or false (F)?

1 Paulo had fun at the football match. _____
2 Paulo turned off the video. _____

2 Match the words in the lists below.

- me — himself
- you (😊) — ourselves
- him — itself
- her — myself
- it — yourself
- we — herself
- you (😊😊+) — themselves
- them — yourselves

(me is matched to myself)

3 Match the sentences below with the pictures.

1 They painted each other. • • a 
2 They painted themselves. • • b 
3 They painted it themselves. • • c

4 Complete the sentences with **each other** or reflexive pronouns and the verbs below.

buy   cut   look   teach   wave

1 Don't _____ cut yourself _____!

2 She's _____ at _____ in the mirror.

3 They're _____ to _____.

4 You should _____ a new car.

5 I'm _____ Japanese.

CHECK YOUR ANSWERS AND STUDY THE INFORMATION ON PAGE 70.

5 Complete the conversations below. Use emphatic pronouns.

1. Who repaired Paulo's video?
   Paulo and Carlos _repaired it themselves._

2. Mum, make me a sandwich.
   I'm busy. Make _____

3. Who did your homework? It's very good!
   I _____

4. Who painted your house?
   Tony and I _____

5. We can carry the bags, Dad.
   They're too heavy. You can't _____

6. Open the door for the dog.
   No. It can _____

7. Who cut her hair? It's beautiful!
   She _____

8. Did you pay for his lunch?
   No, he _____

6 Use **each other** or reflexive/emphatic pronouns to complete the story.

1. I wanted to watch _myself_ on my holiday, but the video's broken. Who broke it?

2. Paulo and Carlos pointed at _____ .

3. The video didn't break _____ . So who broke it?

4. We don't know who broke it, but we wanted to help. So we repaired it _____ .

5. And now you're going to take the video to the repair shop and pay for it _____ too!

7 Use words from exercise 2 to write positive and negative sentences about you, your friends and your family. Write about the things below.

1 cut hair   2 do homework   3 repair the TV
4 buy clothes   5 cook dinner   6 paint the house

Examples:
I (don't) cut my hair myself.
1 _____
2 _____
3 _____
4 _____
5 _____
6 _____

PUZZLE

Ann and Bill have got broken arms. They are very hungry because they can't feed themselves. What should they do?

_____

17 I used to forget everything!

1a Read the advert for the book **Think Clearly**.

b Are these sentences true (T) or false (F)?

1 Carol has a bad memory. _____
2 Carol had a bad memory. _____
3 Carol hated studying. _____
4 Carol hates studying. _____

c Read the sentence and choose the correct timeline.

Studying used to be a problem. _____

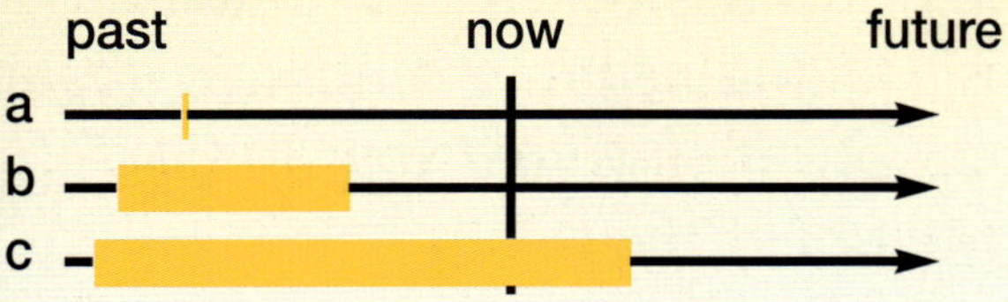

past   now   future
a
b
c

Think Clearly is a new book to help you learn better! Do you forget things? Carol Baker used to have a bad memory before she found out about *Think Clearly*. This is her letter to us:

Studying used to be difficult. I didn't use to enjoy it. I used to forget everything! Then last year I read *Think Clearly*. Now learning is easy and it's fun.

We spoke to Carol:

- Carol, did you use to enjoy school?
- No, I didn't. I used to hate it because I had a terrible memory.
- What did you use to forget?
- Numbers, people's names, everything! One year, I forgot my mother's birthday!

2a Complete the sentences from the advert.

+ I _____ forget everything!
− I _____ enjoy it.
? _____ you _____ enjoy school?
  _____ you _____ forget?

b Now complete the sentences below.

+ Carol _____ hate studying.
− She _____ remember things.
? _____ she _____ forget names?
  _____ she _____ hate?

▶▶ CHECK YOUR ANSWERS AND STUDY THE INFORMATION ON PAGES 70–71.

---

3 Look at the pictures and write affirmative sentences with **used to** about people 50,000 years ago. Use the verbs below.

eat   live   ~~sleep~~   travel   use   wear

1 They used to sleep on the ground.
2 _____
3 _____
4 _____
5 _____
6 _____

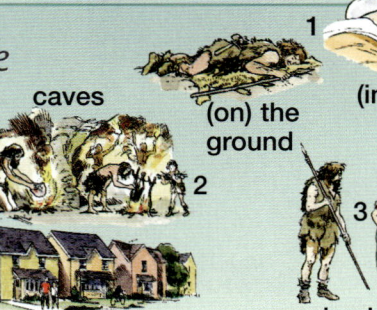

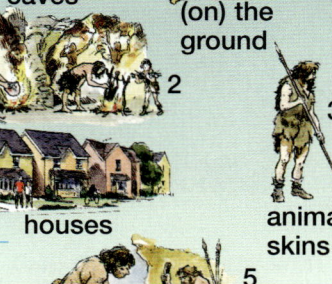

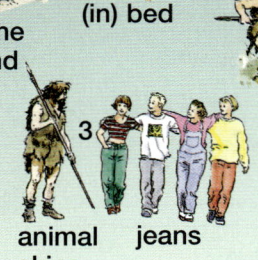

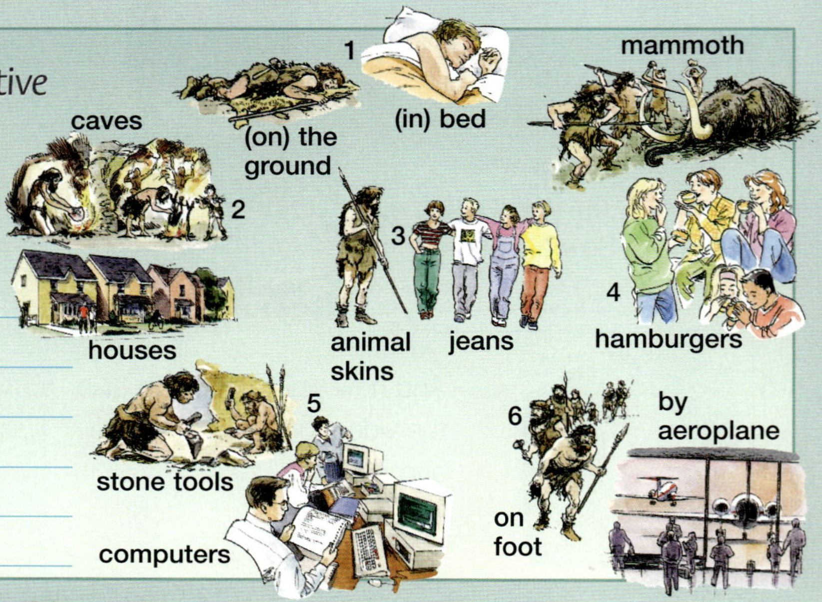

1 (on) the ground / (in) bed — caves / mammoth
2 houses
3 animal skins / jeans
4 hamburgers
5 stone tools / computers
6 by aeroplane / on foot

4 Look at the pictures in exercise 3 again and write negative sentences with **used to** about people 50,000 years ago.

1 They didn't use to sleep in beds.
2 _____
3 _____
4 _____
5 _____
6 _____

5 Read Carol Baker's school report. Write questions with **used to** and short answers about Carol at school.

SCHOOL REPORT: Carol Baker – summer 1992

Music	C	Carol sings beautifully but forgets the words.
English	B	Carol enjoys reading but doesn't like writing.
Sports	A	Carol enjoys tennis and does well.
Maths	D	Carol doesn't understand maths and should ask more questions.
Geography	D	Carol studies hard but doesn't remember places.

1 Did she use to sing beautifully?
  Yes, she did.
2 _____ writing?
3 _____ tennis?
4 _____ maths?
5 _____ places?

6 Complete the conversation. Use the past simple or **used to** and the verbs below.

~~be~~ be be do
give hate play wear

MUM: Don't shout, Kim!
KIM: Sorry, Mum.
MUM: She _didn't use to be_ (1) noisy. She _____ (2) speaking to people.
LIAM: _____ she _____ (3) shy?
MUM: Yes, she did!
LIAM: What _____ she _____ (4)?
MUM: She _____ (5) quietly with her dolls. Then her uncle Tom _____ (6) her a drum kit for her birthday.
LIAM: How old _____ (7) she?
MUM: Seven. She _____ (8) beautiful clothes too.
KIM: Oh, Mum, please! Come on, Liam. Let's go!

7 Can you remember yourself at four years old? How were you different then? Write affirmative and negative sentences with **used to** about you.

1 _____
2 _____
3 _____
4 _____
5 _____

PUZZLE Match the sentence parts to make three funny jokes.

I used to forget everything • • but then I fell in the basin!
I used to be a tap dancer • • was a pet with a jumper on in summer.
I used to think that a hot dog • • but now I ... I ... er ...

18 I won't be able to live without you

1a Read the story from the comic.

Prince, the police dog, is dying. Yesterday, the Bad Brothers stole the secret plans for space project X. Prince chased them to their car but he couldn't catch them. Then the Bad Brothers drove their car at Prince. He couldn't run fast enough – and they hit him.

Only Professor Jacobs can help Prince. He's a scientist. He builds robots.

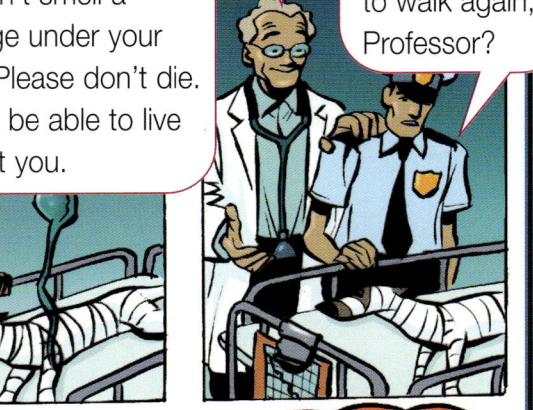

Oh Prince! You could smell the Bad Brothers from 200 metres. Now you can't smell a sausage under your nose. Please don't die. I won't be able to live without you.

Don't worry, Officer. We can save him. We can rebuild him.

Will he be able to walk again, Professor?

Yes, he will. Next week, he'll be able to run at 200 kilometres an hour. He'll be able to see at night. He'll be ...

Robodog!

b Match the pictures of Prince with the times.

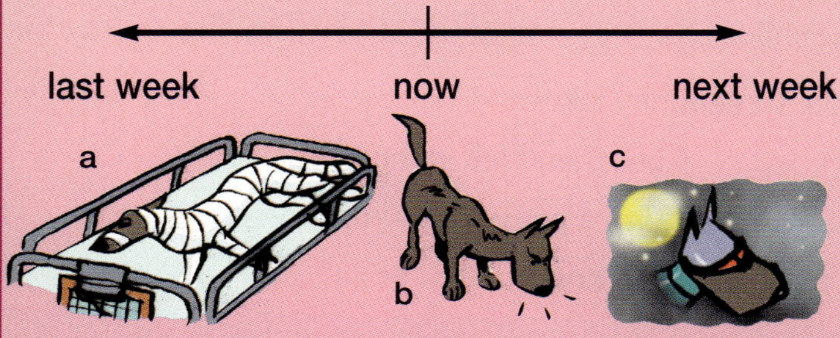

last week ———— now ———— next week

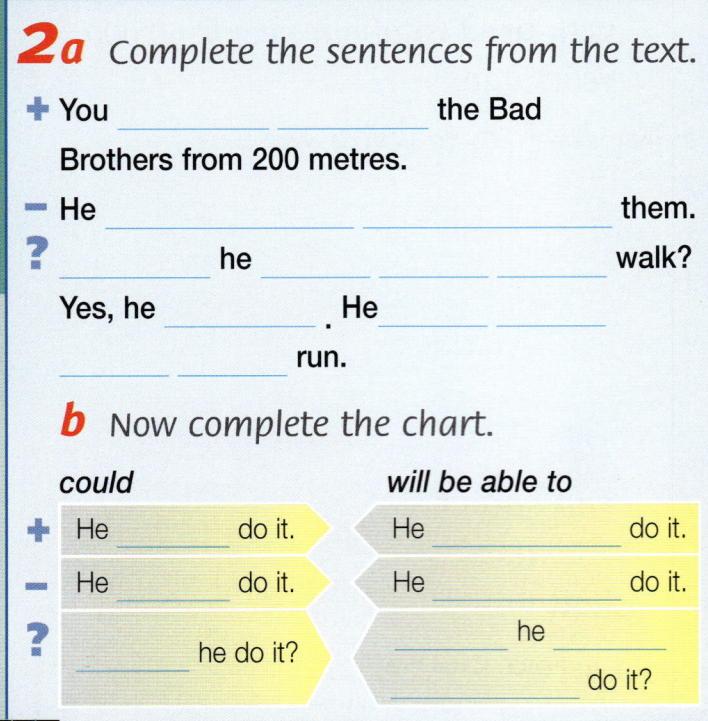

a   b   c

2a Complete the sentences from the text.

+ You _____ _____ the Bad Brothers from 200 metres.
− He _____ them.
? _____ he _____ walk?
Yes, he _____. He _____ _____ run.

b Now complete the chart.

	could		will be able to	
+	He ____ do it.		He ____ do it.	
−	He ____ do it.		He ____ do it.	
?	____ he do it?		____ he ____ do it?	

➡️ CHECK YOUR ANSWERS AND STUDY THE INFORMATION ON PAGE 71.

3 Write sentences about Robodog. Use **will/won't be able to** and the verbs below.

catch   fly   jump   run   save   swim

1 He'll be able to run fast.
2 _____
3 _____
4 _____
5 _____ the plans.
6 _____ the Bad Brothers.

4 A cyclist hit Eric's cat. Eric is talking to the vet. Write Eric's questions with **will be able to**.

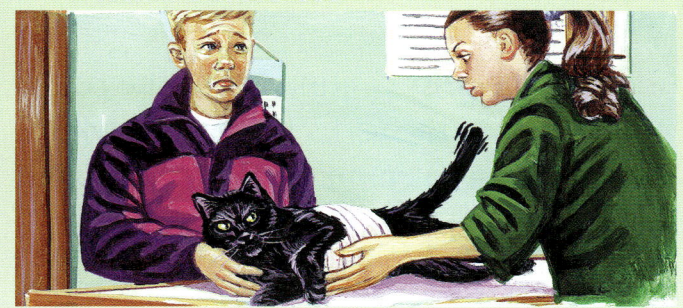

1 Will she be able to walk?
Not for a day or two, but then she'll start walking again.
2 _____
Yes, her eyes are OK.
3 _____
Oh, yes. She can hear now – her ears are moving.
4 _____
Not today, but you'll be able to take her home tomorrow.

5 Write sentences about Professor Jacobs at four years old. Use the words below and **could/couldn't**.

1 He could make models.
2 _____
3 _____
4 _____
5 _____
6 _____

6 Use the verbs in exercise 5 to ask a friend in your class questions about him or her at four years old.

1 Could you make models?
2 _____
3 _____
4 _____
5 _____
6 _____

7 Now answer the questions in exercise 6 about you at four years old.

1 _____
2 _____
3 _____
4 _____
5 _____
6 _____

PUZZLE

Police officers Andrews (A), Brown (B) and Clark (C) were chasing Dick (D) and Ernie (E), the terrible twins. They ran into a building. No one could see everyone. Read the information and write A, B, C, D or E on the people in the plan.

A could see B and E.   D couldn't see A and B.
B could see A.   E couldn't see B and C.
C could see D.   B could see the door.

Check point 13–18

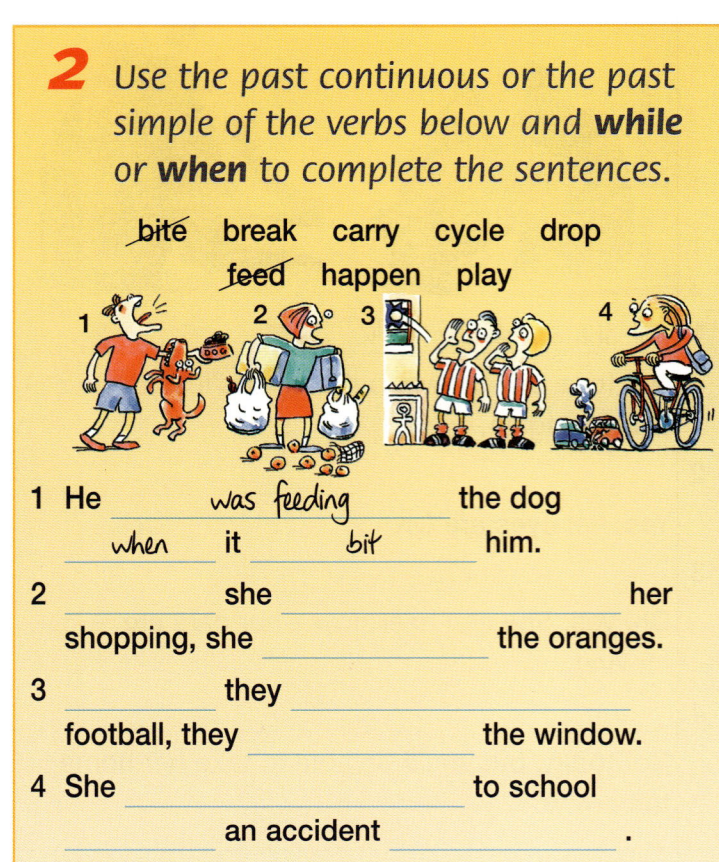

1 Write the questions and answers. Use the past continuous and the verbs below.

argue   ~~look at~~   play   read   sleep

1 What was he doing at 4 o'clock?
  He was looking at the paintings.
2
3
4
5
6

2 Use the past continuous or the past simple of the verbs below and **while** or **when** to complete the sentences.

~~bite~~   break   carry   cycle   drop
~~feed~~   happen   play

1 He ___was feeding___ the dog ___when___ it ___bit___ him.
2 _____ she _____ her shopping, she _____ the oranges.
3 _____ they _____ football, they _____ the window.
4 She _____ to school _____ an accident _____.

3 Use **who** or **which** and the verbs below to complete the information about people and things.

climb   fly   invent   run   see

1 Hubble is the telescope _____ furthest in space.
2 Galileo was the scientist _____ the telescope.
3 Hillary and Tenzing were the climbers _____ first _____ Everest.
4 *Concorde* is the aeroplane _____ the fastest.
5 Bannister was the runner _____ first _____ a mile (about 1500 metres) in under four minutes.

4 Put the words in the correct order to make sentences and add a reflexive/emphatic pronoun or **each other**.

1 washing   It's
   It's washing itself.

2 it   made   I

3 can't   repair   She   it

4 dinner   their   They're making

5 radio   heard   the   He   on

6 love   They

5 Complete the sentences with affirmative or negative forms of **used to** and the verbs below.

~~exercise~~   live   play   take   walk   watch

1 Before she went swimming every week, she didn't use to exercise.

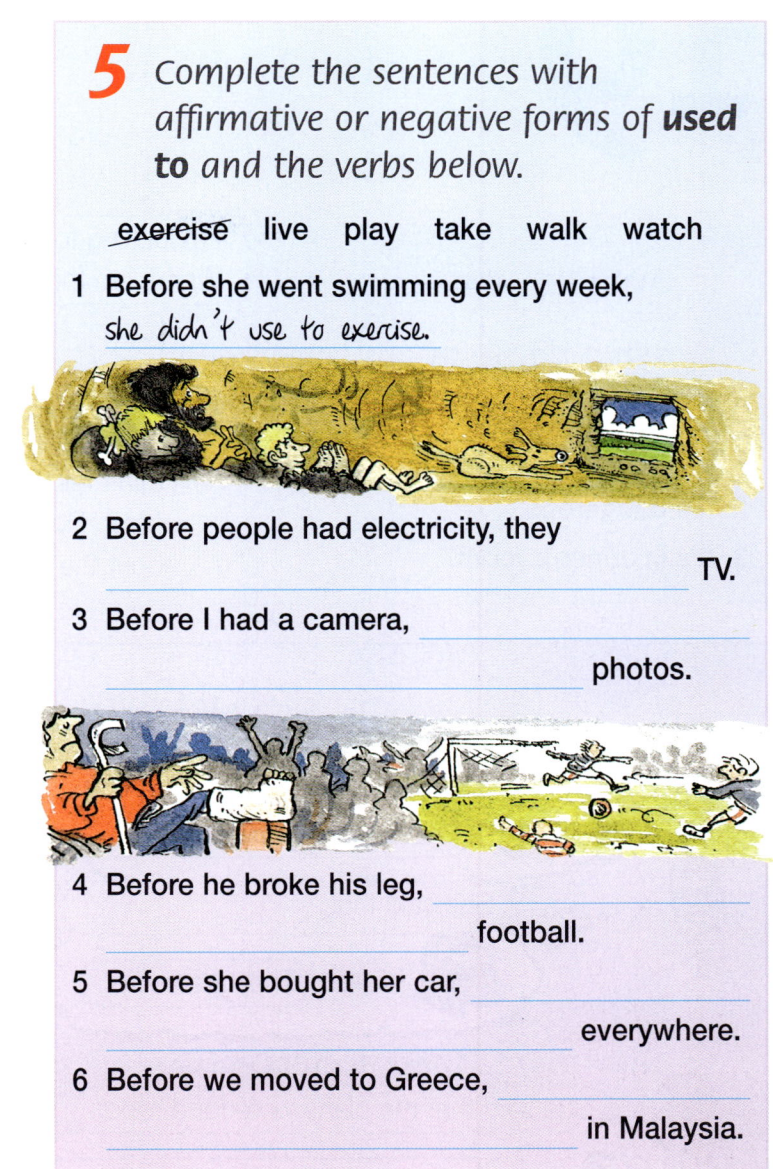

2 Before people had electricity, they _____ TV.

3 Before I had a camera, _____ photos.

4 Before he broke his leg, _____ football.

5 Before she bought her car, _____ everywhere.

6 Before we moved to Greece, _____ in Malaysia.

6 Mary is four years old. Look at the timeline and complete the sentences about her with **could** or **couldn't** or **will** or **won't be able to**.

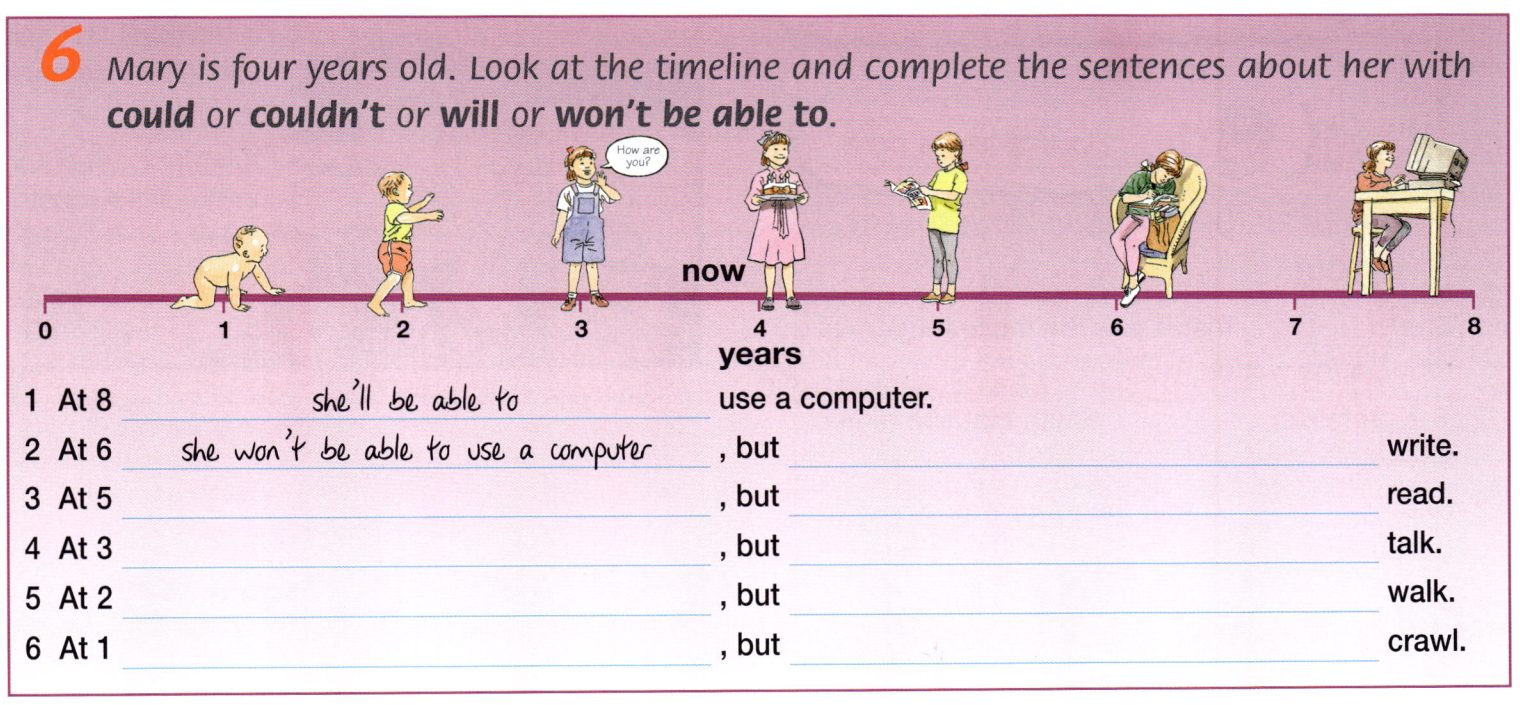

1 At 8   she'll be able to   use a computer.
2 At 6   she won't be able to use a computer , but _____ write.
3 At 5   _____ , but _____ read.
4 At 3   _____ , but _____ talk.
5 At 2   _____ , but _____ walk.
6 At 1   _____ , but _____ crawl.

19 Smith asked her where the robot was

1a Read the story.

b What do Smith and Jones know about the robot? Tick (✓) or cross (✗).

1 It's big. _____
2 It's dangerous. _____
3 It's in Jones's room. _____

I'm looking for the plans. Where are they?

I can't tell you. They're secret. How do know about the plans?

Do you know Professor X?

I am Professor X!

Jones is writing his report.

Smith: I asked her where the plans were. She said that she couldn't tell me. She said that they were secret. Then I asked her if she knew Professor X. She said 'I am Professor X!' So I asked her about the secret plans again.
Jones: What did she say?
Smith: She told me that they were for a very large robot. She said that it was the most dangerous robot in the world!

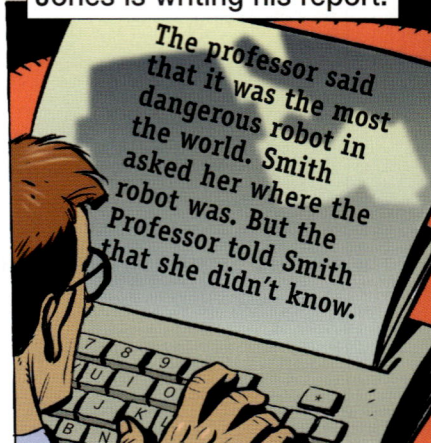

The professor said that it was the most dangerous robot in the world. Smith asked her where the robot was. But the Professor told Smith that she didn't know.

2a Rewrite these sentences from the story.

1 *She said that she couldn't tell me.*
   I _____

2 *She said that _____*
   They are secret.

Now rewrite these sentences.

3 *She said that the plans were for a robot.*
   The plans _____

4 _____ said that _____
   I'm looking for the plans.

b Complete these sentences with **said** or **told**.

1 She _____ that it was the most dangerous robot in the world!
2 The professor _____ Smith that she didn't know.
3 She _____ us that the robot was dangerous.
4 She _____ that it was very large.

CHECK YOUR ANSWERS AND STUDY THE INFORMATION ON PAGE 72.

3 Jones is phoning Smith. Complete Smith's report.

(1) The robot is in my room. (2) It's looking at me. (3) I can see Professor X. (4) She's turning off the robot!

1 Jones said _that the robot was in his room._
2 He told _____
3 He said _____
4 He told _____

4 Rewrite Smith's questions from the story.

1 [speech bubble] I asked her where the plans were.

2 "Do you know Professor X?"
   I asked _____

Now rewrite these questions.

3 Smith asked her where the robot was.
   [speech bubble] _____

4 Smith asked _____
   "Is it dangerous?"

▶▶ CHECK YOUR ANSWERS AND STUDY THE INFORMATION ON PAGE 72.

5 Write these sentences with reported speech.

1 She asked me, 'Where are you going?'
   She asked me where I was going.

2 'Do you want a drink?' he asked me.
   _____

3 They asked her, 'What do you want?'
   _____

4 'Why are you asking?' she asked them.
   _____

5 He asked him, 'Can you play the piano?'
   _____

6 'Does he remember the song?' he asked her.
   _____

6 Write Sue and Eric's conversation with reported speech.

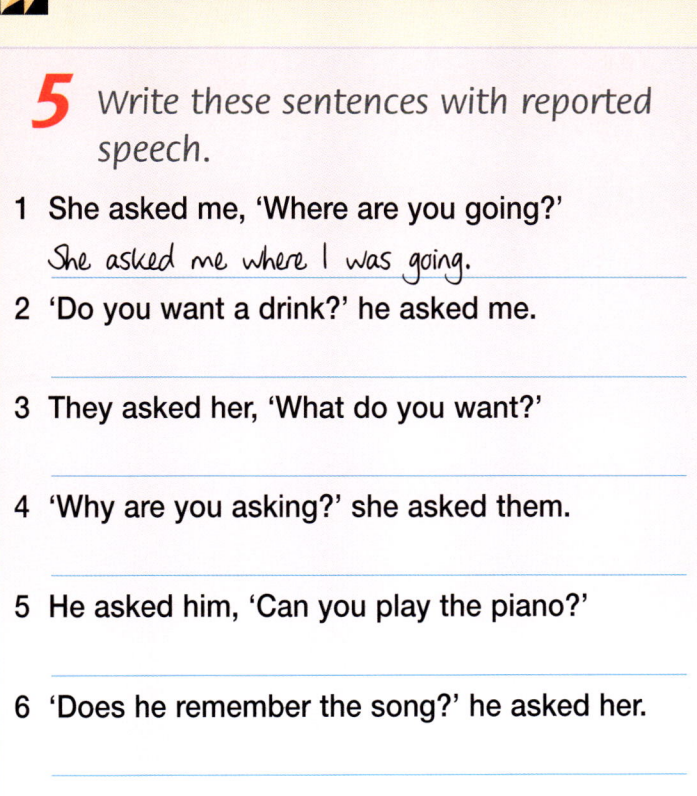

"Where's Kim?" "Can you see her?"
"I can't see her anywhere."

1 *Sue asked where Kim was.*
2 _____
3 _____

"I can see her." "Where is she?"
"She's playing with the band."

4 _____
5 _____
6 _____

7 What interesting things did people say to you or ask yesterday? Use reported speech.

1 My friend told _____
2 _____
3 _____
4 _____

PUZZLE

My friend works at a hospital. He told me that a man brought his son to the hospital because he was very ill. But the doctor saw the boy and said, 'He's my son!' My friend asked me if I knew why.

Do you understand the story?

20 You must come home at 10.30

1a Read James's conversation with his mum.

JAMES: Mum, there's a late film at the cinema tonight. It's a good horror film. Can I go?

MUM: Yes, James, but you must come home at 10.30.

JAMES: But ...

MUM: James, you have to get up at 5 o'clock tomorrow. You're going fishing with your granddad.

JAMES: Please, Mum. Can I stay to 12.00?

MUM: Can you remember the last time you went fishing with your granddad? You were two hours late. You mustn't be late again.

JAMES: But Elena, Liam and Sue are going to stay to 12.00.

MUM: Yes, but they don't have to get up at 5 o'clock tomorrow morning.

b Answer the questions about the conversation.

1 Is James going to the cinema? _____
2 Is James going to stay late? _____
3 What time is James going to get up tomorrow morning? _____

2a Read the sentences from the conversation. In which sentence does **can** = ability? In which one does **can** = permission?

1 **Can** you remember the last time you went fishing? _____
2 **Can** I stay late? _____

b Read the sentences below. Can James choose the times? Write **yes** or **no**.

1 You **must** come home at 10.30. _____
2 You **have to** get up at 5 o'clock. _____

c Read the sentences below. Can James / his friends choose the times? Write **yes** or **no**.

1 You **mustn't** be late. _____
2 Elena, Liam and Sue **don't have to** get up early in the morning. _____

3a Complete the sentences from the conversation.

1 You _____ come home at 10.30.
2 You _____ be late.
3 You _____ get up early.
4 They _____ get up at 5 o'clock.

b Now put these words in the correct order and make sentences.

1 | get | enough sleep | You | must |

2 | at 12.00 | You | come home | mustn't |

3 | have to | your grandad | meet | You |

4 | They | come home | don't have to | at 10.30 |

CHECK YOUR ANSWERS AND STUDY THE INFORMATION ON PAGES 72–73.

4 Complete the answers to the questions. Use **can** or **can't** short answers and **must** or **mustn't**.

1. Mum, can I have some money?
   Yes, _you can_. But you _mustn't_ spend it on sweets.
2. Mum, can I go out?
   No, _____. You _____ do your homework.
3. Mum, can I put on the TV?
   No, _____. You _____ be quiet. Your father is sleeping.
4. Mum, can I go to the cinema?
   Yes, _____. But you _____ finish your homework first.
5. Mum, can I have a hamburger?
   No, _____. You _____ eat junk food.

5 Complete the sentences with **have/has to** or **don't/doesn't have to**. Use the verbs below.

get up   go   pay   stay   wait   walk

1. It's Monday morning. She _has to go_ to school.
2. She's ill. She _____ in bed.
3. He's 12 years old. He _____.
4. They've got bikes. They _____ to school.
5. You can't go. You _____ at the traffic lights.
6. Today is Sunday. She _____ early.

6 Sue works in a café at weekends. Complete her sentences with **must/mustn't**, **have to/don't have to** and the verbs below.

be   be   drop   speak   wear   work

1. I _mustn't be_ late.
2. The café doesn't open on Sunday afternoons, so I _____.
3. I _____ a white shirt.
4. I _____ the plates.
5. I _____ careful in the kitchen.
6. I _____ politely all the time!

7 Write about you. Use **must/mustn't**, **have to/don't have to**.

1. _____ go to school on Sundays.
2. _____ be careful at busy roads.
3. _____ wash the dishes.
4. _____ be late for school.
5. _____ miss lessons.
6. _____ study English.

PUZZLE

Annette must see Bernice quickly. She can use a small road in the countryside which is 30 km. She doesn't have to use it because there's a new road which is 15 km. But she has to wait 10 minutes with the other cars to pay to use the new road. She mustn't drive faster than 60 km an hour. How long will her journey take? Which is the faster road?

21 The work has been hard

1a Read about the Water Project.

Anoma has just taken water from the new well. She and the other villagers used to walk 7 km for their water before the Water Project. The Water Project has already built four wells in other villages; this one is the fifth. The Water Project has given the money for the wells, but the villagers have done the work themselves. The work has been hard but now there is water for everyone.

Anoma's friend, Eniye, lives 3 kilometres from Anoma's village. The people haven't built a well in Eniye's village, but the Project workers are going to help them. They haven't started the well yet, but Eniye knows that life will be easier with clean water. She has seen the change in Anoma's life!

b Answer the questions.
1 How many new wells are there? _____
2 Has Eniye's village got a well? _____
3 Was building the wells easy? _____

3a Complete the sentences from the text in exercise 1.
+ The villagers _____ _____ the work.
+ The work _____ _____ hard.
− The people _____ a well.

b Now use the correct forms of **have**, **be** and **build** to complete these sentences about the text.
+ The people in Anoma's village _____ _____ a well.
− The work _____ _____ easy.

➤➤ CHECK YOUR ANSWERS AND STUDY THE INFORMATION ON PAGES 73–74.

2 Complete the table below with verb forms from the text.

infinitive	past simple	past participle
be	was/were	been
build	built	
do	did	
give	gave	
see	saw	
start	started	
take	took	

4 Look at the notes for the School Building Project. Use the present perfect to write affirmative or negative sentences.

Project workers	Teacher
1 build school ✓	4 buy books ✗
2 paint school ✓	5 speak to parents ✓
3 make tables and chairs ✗	6 meet the students ✓

1 They *have built the school.*
2 _____
3 _____
4 She _____
5 _____
6 _____

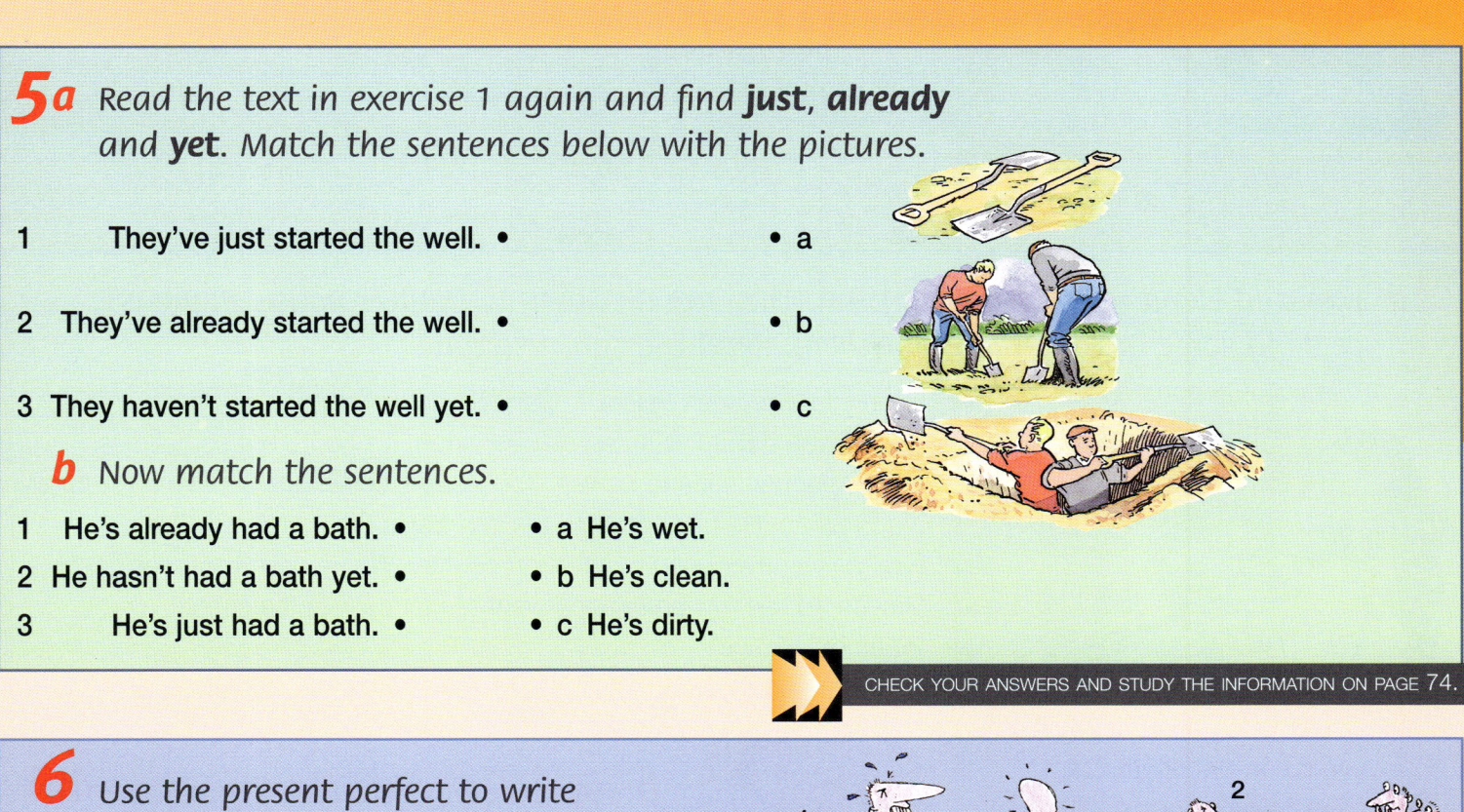

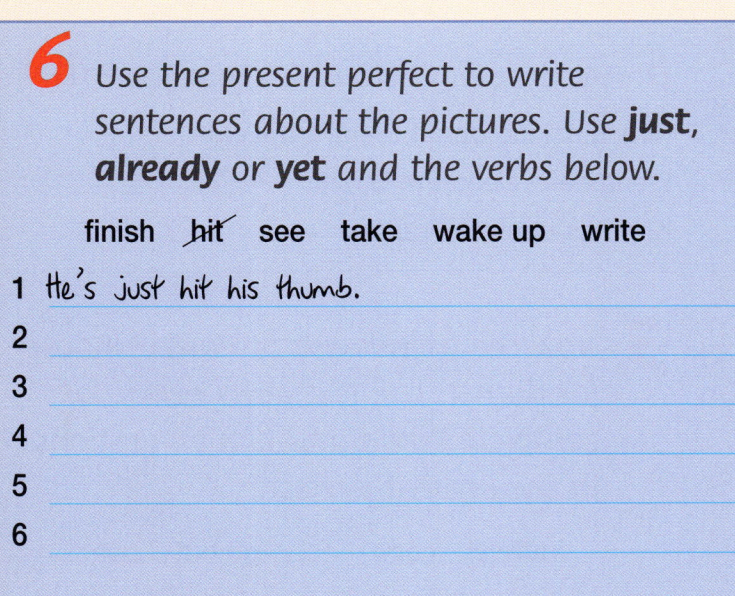

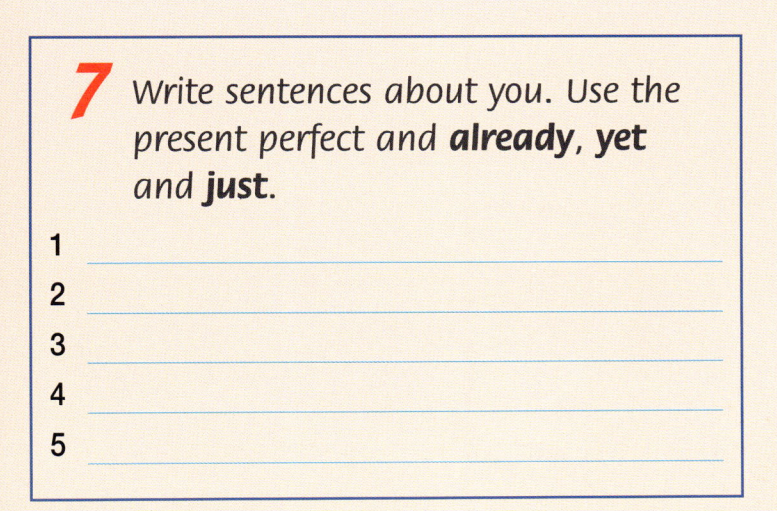

5a
Read the text in exercise 1 again and find **just**, **already** and **yet**. Match the sentences below with the pictures.

1 They've just started the well. •
2 They've already started the well. •
3 They haven't started the well yet. •

• a
• b
• c

b
Now match the sentences.

1 He's already had a bath. •   • a He's wet.
2 He hasn't had a bath yet. •   • b He's clean.
3 He's just had a bath. •   • c He's dirty.

➤➤ CHECK YOUR ANSWERS AND STUDY THE INFORMATION ON PAGE 74.

6
Use the present perfect to write sentences about the pictures. Use **just**, **already** or **yet** and the verbs below.

finish   hit   see   take   wake up   write

1 He's just hit his thumb.
2 _____
3 _____
4 _____
5 _____
6 _____

PUZZLE
Abi's necklace has just broken and some of the beads have fallen off. Abi knows the order of the beads. Can you draw the beads in the correct places?

7
Write sentences about you. Use the present perfect and **already**, **yet** and **just**.

1 _____
2 _____
3 _____
4 _____
5 _____

22 Where have you put the chocolates?

1a Kim and Elena are waiting for Liam. They are all going to Paulo's house. Paulo is cooking some Brazilian food for them. Read the conversation.

KIM: Have you ever been to Brazil, Elena?
ELENA: No, I haven't. But I've eaten Brazilian food. It's good, but sometimes there's pepper in it and it's very hot. Paulo's cooking is excellent. His family are Brazilian. He often goes to the carnival in Rio.
KIM: Really! I've never been to a foreign country. Where have you been?
ELENA: Greece, to see my family and I went to France with the school.
KIM: When did you go?
ELENA: Two years ago, before I met you.

ELENA: It's time to go. Have you finished your homework yet, Liam?
LIAM: Yes, I have. I've just finished it.
ELENA: OK, let's go. Where have you put the chocolates for Paulo?
LIAM: Oh! Were the chocolates for Paulo?

b Are the sentences true (T) or false (F)?
1 Kim is asking about Elena's travels. _____
2 Elena hasn't been to Brazil. _____
3 Kim has been to France. _____

2a Put the words below in the correct order and make sentences from the conversation.

1 | finished | your homework | you | Have |
_____?
2 | have | I | Yes, |
_____.
3 | put | the chocolates | have | Where | you |
_____?

b Now complete the sentences with the verbs **finish** and **eat**.

1 _____ Elena and Kim _____ their homework?
2 Yes, _____.
3 _____ _____ _____ the chocolates? Liam has!

3 Now the friends are at Paulo's house for dinner. Use the verbs below to complete Paulo and Kim's questions in the present perfect.

~~arrive~~   cook   eat   go out   use

KIM: (1) _Have_ we _arrived_ early?
KIM: (2) _____ you _____ pepper?
KIM: (3) What _____ you _____?
KIM: (4) _____ your parents _____?
PAULO: (5) Who _____ the chocolates?

CHECK YOUR ANSWERS AND STUDY THE INFORMATION ON PAGE 75.

4a Complete these sentences from the conversation in exercise 1.

1 Have you _____ been to Brazil?
2 I've _____ been to a foreign country.

b Now complete these sentences.

1 Have you _____ eaten Paulo's cooking?
2 I've _____ eaten Brazilian food.

c Match the pictures with the questions.

a    b

1 Have you ever been to Spain? ____
2 Have you been to Spain? ____

CHECK YOUR ANSWERS AND STUDY THE INFORMATION ON PAGE 75.

5 These are Liam's holiday photos. Write Liam's questions and his friend's short answers. Use **ever** and the verbs below.

eat   play   ride   stay   swim

1 Have you ever eaten fish and chips ?
No, I haven't.
I don't like fish.

2 _____ ?
_____
But I've ridden a horse.

3 _____ ?
_____
I swam in the Mediterranean last year.

4 _____ ?
_____
But I've been camping.

5 _____ ?
_____
I play with my friend.

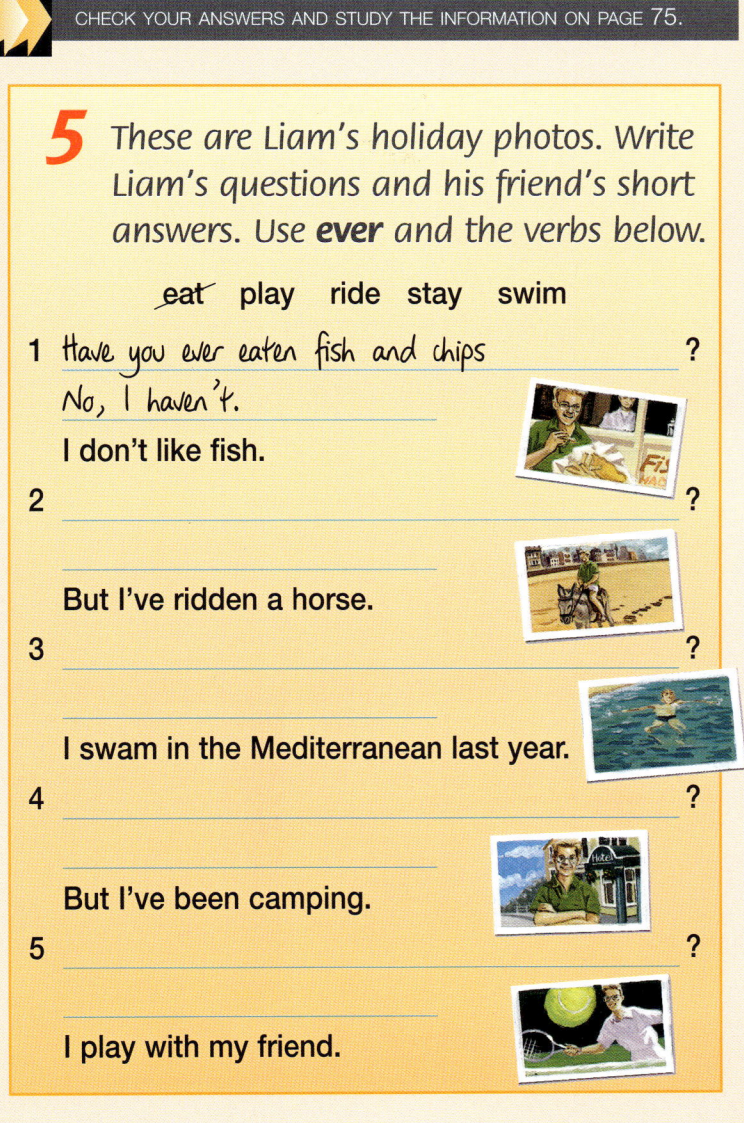

6 Complete the letter with the verbs below. Use the present perfect or past simple. Choose **ever**, **never** or **yet**.

~~break~~   break   buy   go   go   pay   plan   watch

Dear Amanda
I can't go skiing with you next month. I 've broken (1) my leg! Have you ever / yet _____ (2) your leg? I _____ (3) some skis last week. I can't believe it! I _____ never / ever _____ (4) skiing, but I _____ (5) it on TV. _____ you _____ (6) for the holiday never / yet? My friend Lisa _____ (7) skiing last year. She's very good. She _____ (8) her holiday yet / ever.
So she can go with you! What do you think?
Love, Jill

7 Write answers to the questions about you.

1 Have you ever ridden a camel?
_____

2 Have you seen a film this week?
_____

3 Have you ever told anyone a secret?
_____

4 Have you eaten lunch yet?
_____

5 Have you read a newspaper today?
_____

PUZZLE

Bert has just made this shape from one piece of paper. Which one has he used?

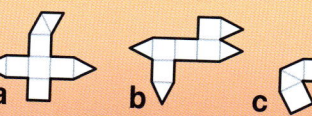

a   b    c

23 If he isn't fit, he won't play in the big match

1a Read the newspaper report.

Next Saturday, the two best teams in England will play in the football final of the All England Trophy. Yesterday, Chelsea played Leeds in the first semi-final game and Chelsea won 3–1. Tomorrow, Derby are playing Stoke in the second semi-final. Derby are a strong team, and most people think that they will win. They'll play Chelsea next Saturday if they win tomorrow. If Derby win the final, they'll keep the trophy for the second year. And Chelsea's star player has been to hospital about his left knee. If he isn't fit, he won't play in the big match.

SEMI-FINALS
CHELSEA 3   v   LEEDS 1
DERBY   v   STOKE

Final
CHELSEA   v   _____

b Are the teams below going to play in the final? Write **yes**, **no** or **don't know**.

1 Chelsea _____   3 Leeds _____
2 Stoke _____   4 Derby _____

2a Complete these sentences from the newspaper.

1 They'll play Chelsea _____ they win.
2 _____ he isn't fit _____ he won't play.

b Now complete these sentences.

1 Derby _____ keep the trophy _____ they win the final.
2 _____ Stoke win tomorrow, they _____ Chelsea next week.
3 _____ Stoke don't win tomorrow, they _____ Chelsea next week.

c Are the sentences talking about the past, present or future? _____

3 Match the first parts of the sentences with their second parts below.

1 not work hard   f
2 drive dangerously   _____
3 not take exercise   _____
4 not get up   _____
5 forget umbrella   _____
6 not do homework   _____

a be late for school
b get wet
c have an accident
d teacher be angry
e not get fit
f not pass the exams

4 Now write complete sentences. Use the sentence parts in exercise 3.

1 If she doesn't work hard, she won't pass her exams.
2 _____
3 _____
4 _____
5 _____
6 _____

CHECK YOUR ANSWERS AND STUDY THE INFORMATION ON PAGES 75–76.

5 Complete the sentences with the first conditional.

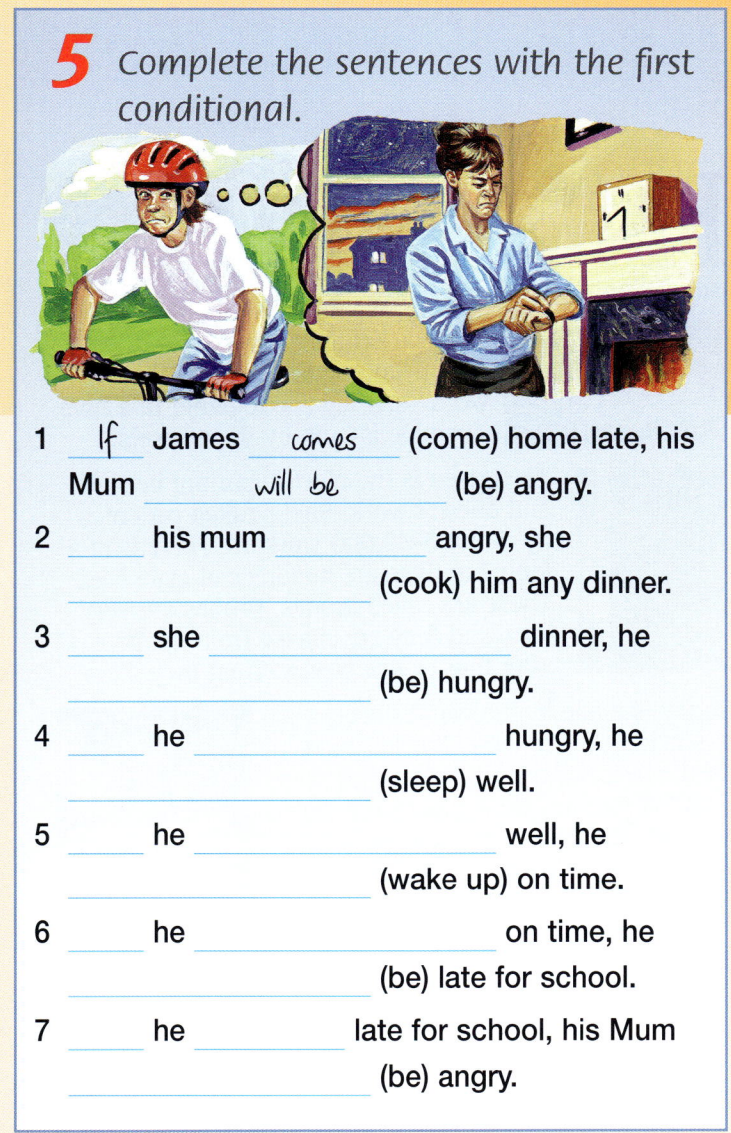

1 _If_ James _comes_ (come) home late, his Mum _will be_ (be) angry.
2 ___ his mum ___ angry, she ___ (cook) him any dinner.
3 ___ she ___ dinner, he ___ (be) hungry.
4 ___ he ___ hungry, he ___ (sleep) well.
5 ___ he ___ well, he ___ (wake up) on time.
6 ___ he ___ on time, he ___ (be) late for school.
7 ___ he ___ late for school, his Mum ___ (be) angry.

6 Write sentences about the pictures. Use the first conditional and the verbs below.

bite   break   catch   chase   ~~cry~~   drop   feed
~~find~~   pay   phone   turn off   wake up

1 If _she doesn't find her dog, she'll cry._
2 If ___
3 The cat ___
4 He ___
5 They ___
6 If ___

7 Write about you.

1 If it rains tomorrow, ___
2 If I have some free time at the weekend, ___
3 If I finish my homework early, ___
4 If I get all my homework right, ___
5 If I feel ill tomorrow, ___
6 If my parents give me some money, ___

PUZZLE

Sally has got a bag of sweets. If she gives half the sweets to one friend, and if she then gives half the sweets in the bag to her other friend, she'll have six sweets for herself in the bag.
How many sweets has she got? ___

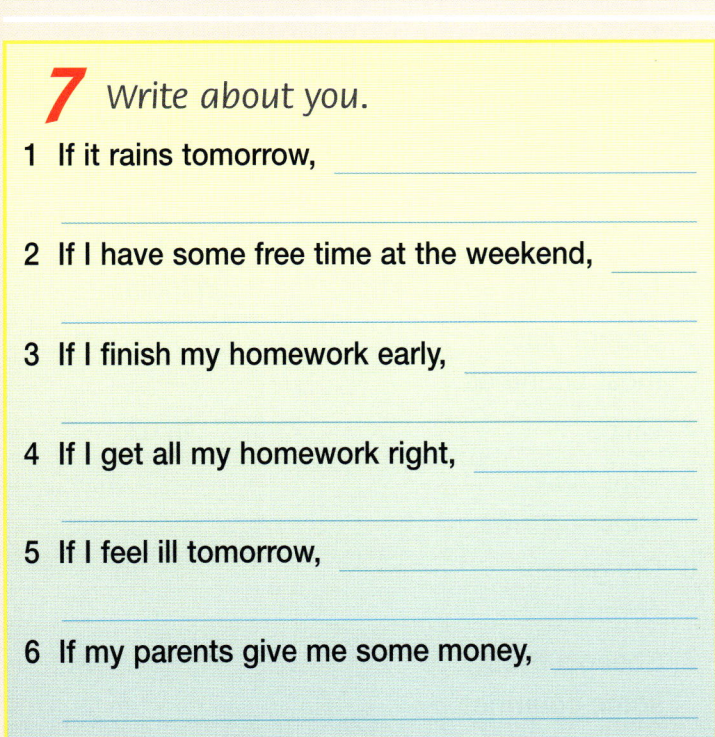

24 Honey is eaten everywhere

Honey Bees are kept by farmers all over the world, and honey is eaten everywhere.

There are three types of Honey Bee; the queen, the drones, and the workers. They live together in a hive. The hive is built by the workers.

The queen is the most important bee and doesn't work. She is taken care of by 50,000–80,000 workers. There isn't a king, but there are hundreds of male bees. These are called drones. Drones are very lazy, and they are chased from the hive after four or five weeks. Then they die.

Honey is made by the worker bees, and it is made from flowers. The bees look for the best flowers, and after they've found them, they do a dance. The dance tells the other workers where to look. Their dance was written about by Karl von Frisch (1886–1982), and now the Bee Dance is understood.

Food

At the hive

1a Read the information about Honey Bees.

b Answer the questions.

1 Who takes care of the queen bee?

2 Which bees make the honey?

3 Who wrote about the Bee Dance?

2a Look at the sentences below. Find the same information in the text and write the sentences.

1 Farmers keep Honey Bees.

2 The worker bees make honey.

3 Karl von Frisch wrote about their dance.

b Now change these sentences.

1 The workers chase the drones.

2 The workers do the work.

3 Karl von Frisch studied bees.

c What are the rules?

CHECK YOUR ANSWERS AND STUDY THE INFORMATION ON PAGE 76.

3 Complete the sentences. Use the verbs below.

cook   drink   eat   fed   grow   ~~make~~   sell

1 Honey ____is made____ in a hive.
2 Tea _____ in India.
3 Orange juice _____ in most countries.
4 Chips _____ in oil.
5 Vegetables _____ in supermarkets.
6 Dry grass _____ to horses.
7 Sheep's eyes _____ in some countries.

4 Rewrite these sentences. Use the passive and **by**.

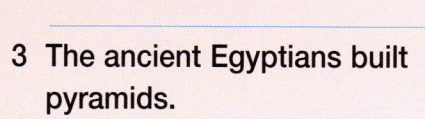

1 Artists paint pictures.
   Pictures are painted by artists.
2 Leonardo painted the Mona Lisa.
   _____
3 The ancient Egyptians built pyramids.
   _____
4 Millions of people visit them every year. 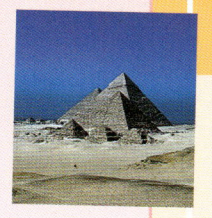
   _____
5 Scientists study the planets.
   _____
6 Galileo invented the telescope. 
   _____
7 The Japanese grow rice.
   _____
8 People everywhere eat rice. 
   _____

5a Complete the sentences from the text in exercise 1.

1 They do _____ dance. _____ dance tells the other workers where to look.
2 They live together in _____ hive. _____ hive is built by the workers.

b Now complete the sentences below.

1 Every hive has got _____ queen. _____ queen is fed by the workers.
2 Karl von Frisch wrote _____ book. _____ book is about bees.

c Why do we use **a** and **the** in these sentences?

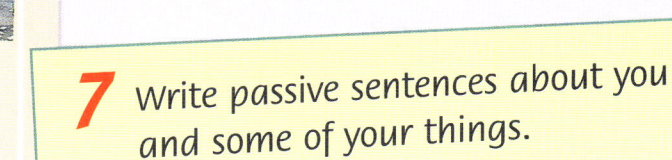

CHECK YOUR ANSWERS ON PAGE 76.

6 Complete the story with the active or passive past simple, and choose **a** or **the**.

Sally's father **bought** (1 buy) a/the farm, and Sally _____ (2 take) to live in the countryside. A/The farm _____ (3 build) near to a/the big forest and it _____ (4 call) Bee Farm. No bees _____ (5 keep) on a/the farm, but she _____ (6 give) honey every day for tea.

Sally's father _____ (7 go) to a/the forest every day. Sally sometimes _____ (8 go) to the forest because she _____ (9 love) the beautiful flowers. One day, she was walking in the forest when a/the very large bee _____ (10 fly) at her. Sally _____ (11 run) and _____ (12 chase) by a/the bee. Suddenly, she _____ (13 see) her father on the ground. 'Sally!' he said. 'I was collecting honey when I _____ (14 fall) out of the tree. I _____ (15 ask) my friend the queen bee to find you. You must help me to get home.'

7 Write passive sentences about you and some of your things.

Examples:
I was born ... . My bike was bought in ...

PUZZLE

Two babies were born on the same day in the same hospital. They had the same parents, but they were not twins! Why not?

Check point 19–24

1 Write the sentences below with reported speech.

1 She told me, 'The answer is easy.'
   She told me that the answer was easy.
2 He said, 'I can't hear you.'
3 She asked me, 'Where do you live?'
4 They said, 'We're twins.'
5 We asked them, 'What are your names?'
6 She said, 'I can speak Spanish.'
7 He told me, 'You are in the wrong class.'

2a Read the library rules. Write sentences with **must/mustn't**.

Library Rules
Please…
- Don't eat in the library
- Don't talk loudly in the library
- Don't play games
- Leave at 5 pm
- Bring books back in 2 weeks
- Don't take the newspapers away
- Bring your library card

1 You mustn't eat.
2
3
4
5
6
7

b Now complete the sentences about the library rules with **mustn't** or **don't have to**.

1 _____ bring books back in one week.
2 _____ eat.
3 _____ leave at 3 pm.

3 Write sentences with the present perfect. Write one sentence with **just**, one with **yet** and one with **already** for each picture.

1 a Flash has already finished.
  b
  c

2 a
  b
  c

3 a
  b
  c

58

4a Amanda is an explorer. Complete the interviewer's questions to Amanda. Use the present perfect, **ever** and the verbs below.

be   climb   ~~eat~~   ride   swim

1 Have you ever eaten sheep's eyes?
2 _____ in the river Nile?
3 _____ to South America?
4 _____ Everest?
5 _____ an elephant?

b Now look at the map of Amanda's travels and write answers about her.

1 Yes she has.
2 _____
3 _____
4 _____
5 _____

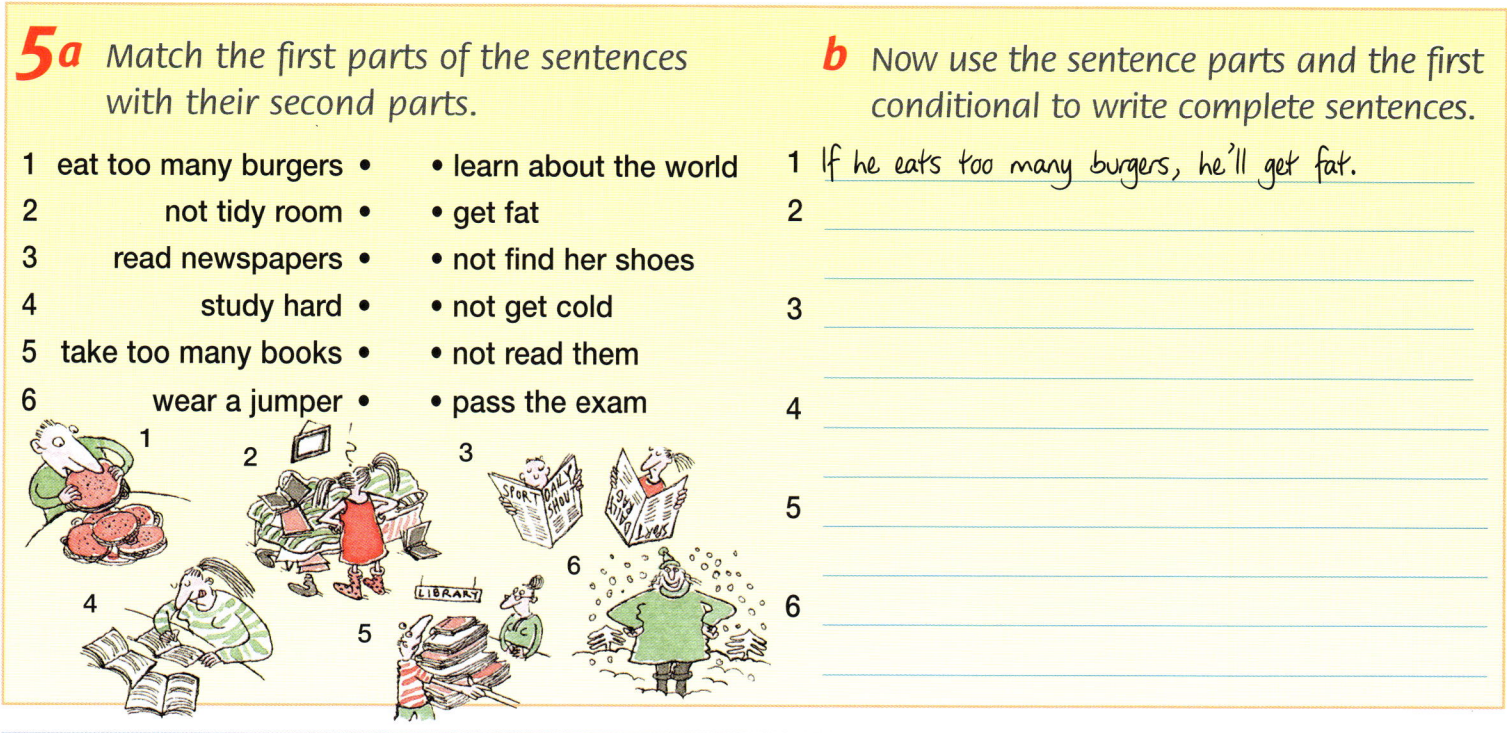

5a Match the first parts of the sentences with their second parts.

1 eat too many burgers • • learn about the world
2 not tidy room • • get fat
3 read newspapers • • not find her shoes
4 study hard • • not get cold
5 take too many books • • not read them
6 wear a jumper • • pass the exam

b Now use the sentence parts and the first conditional to write complete sentences.

1 If he eats too many burgers, he'll get fat.
2 _____
3 _____
4 _____
5 _____
6 _____

6 Complete the sentences with the active and passive past or present simple.

1 The villagers ___built___ (build) a school. The school _____ (paint) by the children.
2 Books _____ (make) from paper, but we _____ (use) trees to make paper.
3 Frank and Ernie _____ (steal) some money, but they _____ (catch) by the police.
4 Coffee _____ (grow) in Brazil, but people everywhere _____ (drink) it.
5 This grammar book _____ (complete). _____ you _____ (speak) English?

Grammar reference

1 Are you lazy or hardworking?

1b 1 Kim 2 Sue 3 James 4 Paulo
2 1 and 2 but 3 or 4 so

Present simple

affirmative

| I/You/We/They | play | an instrument. |
| She/He/It | plays | |

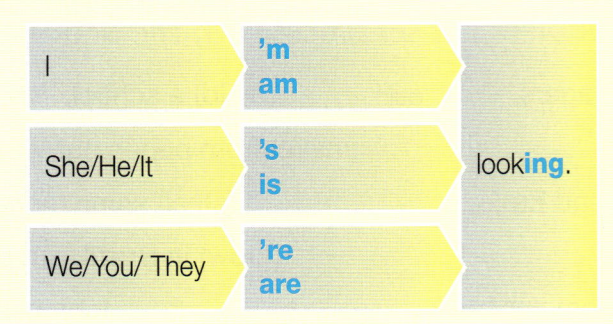

negative

| I/You/We/They | don't play (do not) | an instrument. |
| She/He/It | doesn't play (does not) | |

questions

| Do | I/you/we/they | play | an instrument? |
| Does | she/he/it | | |

Use the present simple for things that happen again and again.

3b 1 loves 2 studies 3 watches 4 plays
c 1 teaches 2 carrries 3 stays 4 likes

Spelling rules – present simple, *he, she, it* (3rd person)
1 + -s
wear + -s wears
2 + -es for words with -ch, -o, -sh, -s, -x or -z
go + -es goes
watch watches
3 ~~y~~ + -ies for words with a consonant + -y
fly + -ies flies

short answers

Yes,	I/you/we/they	do.
	she/he/it	does.
No,	I/you/we/they	don't.
	she/he/it	doesn't.

2 What are they thinking about?

2a
1 They are sitting on a ship.
2 They aren't looking.
3 Is the ship sailing away?
4 What are they thinking about?

b
1 She is holding her baby's hand.
2 The man and woman aren't waving.
3 Is the baby sleeping?
4 Where are they going?

Present continuous

affirmative

I	'm / am	
She/He/It	's / is	looking.
We/You/They	're / are	

60

negative

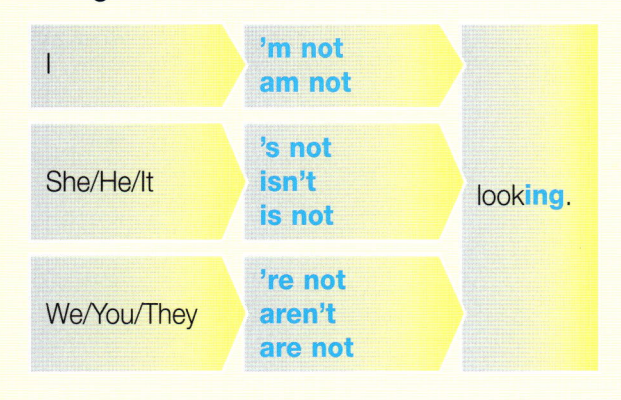

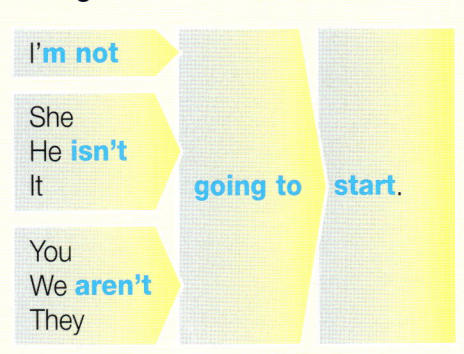

I	'm not / am not	
She/He/It	's not / isn't / is not	looking.
We/You/They	're not / aren't / are not	

questions

Am	I	
Is	she/he/it	looking?
Are	we/you/they	

short answers

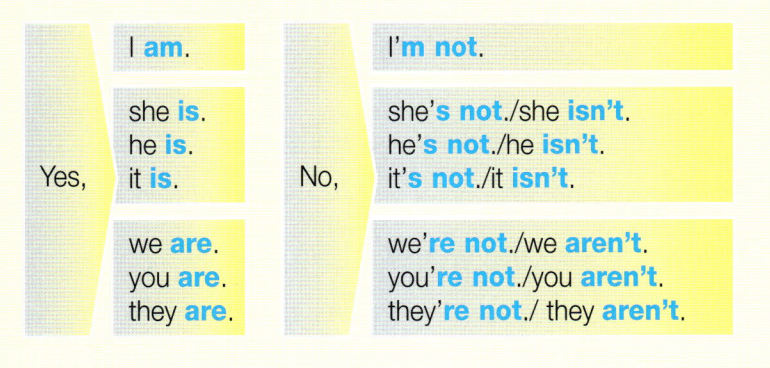

Yes, I **am**. / she **is**. / he **is**. / it **is**. / we **are**. / you **are**. / they **are**.

No, I**'m not**. / she**'s not**./she **isn't**. / he**'s not**./he **isn't**. / it**'s not**./it **isn't**. / we**'re not**./we **aren't**. / you**'re not**./you **aren't**. / they**'re not**./ they **aren't**.

3a 1 looking 2 coming 3 lying 4 sitting
b 1 driving 2 dying 3 jumping 4 running

Use the present continuous for now.

Spelling rules Words ending in:
1 -ie: -ie + -y + -ing   lie → lying
2 -e: -e + -ing   drive → driving
3 a vowel and then a consonant (e.g. -ut, -un, -it), double – × 2 – the consonant + -ing run → running
4 Other words: + -ing   look → looking

3 We're going to start a band

1b No, she doesn't.   2 No, she isn't.

2
+ She**'s going to** get a present.   They **are going to** buy some new clothes.
− She**'s not** / She **isn't going to** dye her hair.   He**'s not** / He **isn't going to** start piano lessons.
? **Is** she **going to** dye her hair?   **Are** they **going to** start a band?

Going to affirmative

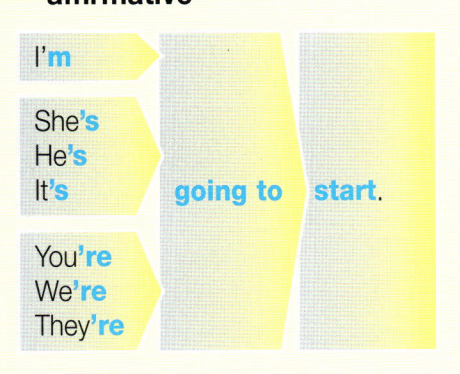

I'm		
She's / He's / It's	going to	start.
You're / We're / They're		

negative

I'm not		
She / He / It isn't	going to	start.
You / We / They aren't		

61

questions

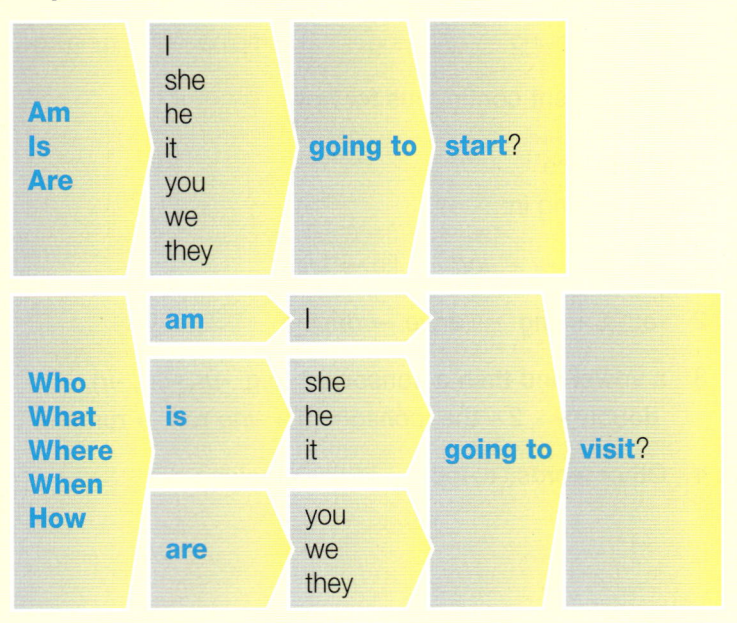

| Am / Is / Are | I / she / he / it / you / we / they | going to | start? |

Who / What / Where / When / How	am	I	going to	visit?
	is	she / he / it		
	are	you / we / they		

short answers

Yes, I am.
Yes, she / he / it is.
Yes, you / we / they are.

No, I 'm not.
No, she / he / it isn't.
No, you / we / they aren't.

Use *be* + *going to* + verb for the future
- you can see the future action; it is starting now
- plans for future actions

4 Did Columbus find the East?

1b
1 moved – move
2 lived – live
3 made – make
4 read – read
5 knew – know
6 thought – think
7 sailed – sail
8 asked – ask
9 agreed – agree
10 found – find

2a
+ He **lived** in Lisbon.
− The Portuguese **didn't believe** him.
? **Did** Columbus **find** the East?
  Why **did** he **take** Spanish ships?

b
+ He found South America.
− He didn't sail East.
? Did he sail West?
  Where did he live?

Past simple regular verbs – spelling rules
1 words ending in -y: -y̶ + -ie + -ed   studied, carried
2 words ending in -e: + -d   liked, moved
3 words with a vowel and then a consonant (for example: -ir, -op, -ip), double – × 2 – the consonant + -ed   stirred, stopped
4 Other words: + -ed   started, looked, watched

be present	*be* past
is	was
isn't	wasn't
are	were
aren't	weren't

Past simple
irregular verbs

begin	**began**	feel	**felt**	lose	**lost**	swim	**swam**
bite	**bit**	find	**found**	make	**made**	take	**took**
break	**broke**	fly	**flew**	meet	**met**	teach	**taught**
bring	**brought**	forget	**forgot**	read	**read**	tell	**told**
build	**built**	get	**got**	ride	**rode**	throw	**threw**
buy	**bought**	give	**gave**	run	**ran**	think	**thought**
come	**came**	go	**went**	see	**saw**	understand	**understood**
do	**did**	grow	**grew**	sell	**sold**	wake up	**woke up**
drink	**drank**	have	**had**	shake	**shook**	win	**won**
drive	**drove**	hit	**hit**	sing	**sang**	write	**wrote**
eat	**ate**	keep	**kept**	sit	**sat**		
fall	**fell**	know	**knew**	speak	**spoke**		
feed	**fed**	leave	**left**	stand	**stood**		

5 Move slowly and carefully

1b 1 yes 2 yes 3 no

2

Adjectives	Adverbs
careful	carefully
comfortable	comfortably
easy	easily
fast	fast
good	well
patient	patiently
quiet	quietly
silent	silently
slow	slowly

3
1 busy – busily
2 dangerous – dangerously
3 beautiful – beautifully
4 simple – simply

happy – happily
brave – bravely
special – specially
gentle – gently

Adverbs – spelling rules

1 adjective ends in -y: -y̶ + -ily
busy + -ily busily
happy happily

2 adjective ends in consonant + -le: -e̶ and + -y
simple + -y simply
comfortable comfortably

3 all other regular adjectives + -ly
brave bravely
careful + -ly carefully
silent silently
slow slowly

⚠ **4** no rule! – some adverbs are irregular
good well
hard hard
fast fast
high high

Adjectives tell us about nouns (people or things).
Adverbs tell us about verbs.

6 Missing meals is bad for you

1b 1 good   2 bad   3 good

2a 1 living   2 Missing   3 Not cooking

b 1 The book is about eating healthy food.
2 Eating healthy food is good for you.
3 Not eating healthy food is bad for you.

- Use nouns and *-ing* forms (= gerunds) for things.

- Gerunds can be subject:
Eating healthy food is good;
or they can be object:
The book is about **eating** healthy food.

- Gerunds can be affirmative or negative:
+ **Missing** meals is bad for you.
− **Not missing** meals is good for you.

- Spelling rules for the *-ing* form: study page 61.

5a Let's **go** swimming.

b 1 Sue **went** swimming last week.
2 Sue **isn't going** swimming.
3 **Does** Sue **go** swimming every week?
4 Sue **didn't go** swimming yesterday.

For leisure activities (but not team games), we often use *go* + gerund:

go camping   go diving   go sailing
go climbing   go fishing   go sightseeing
go cycling   go jogging   go shopping

7 Will you go to Mars?

1b 1 no   2 yes   3 yes

2a
+ They'**ll** (= will) **build** cities on the Moon.
− People **won't** (= will not) **live** outside.
? **Will** you **go** to Mars?
When **will** these things happen?

b
+ People **will travel** to Mars.
− They **won't find** water on the Moon.
? **Will** we **live** in space?
What **will** they **do**?

Future simple *will/won't* + infinitive

affirmative

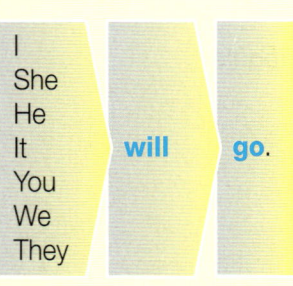

| I / She / He / It / You / We / They | **will** | **go**. |

negative

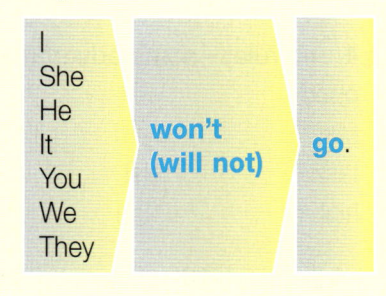

| I / She / He / It / You / We / They | **won't (will not)** | **go**. |

Use *will* for talking about the future
- you know, or think you know
- you can't see the future action starting now

questions

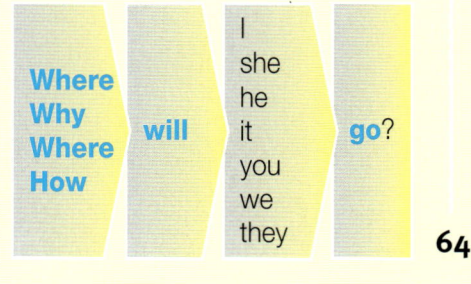

Will I / she / he / it / you / we / they **go**?

Where / Why / Where / How **will** I / she / he / it / you / we / they **go**?

short answers

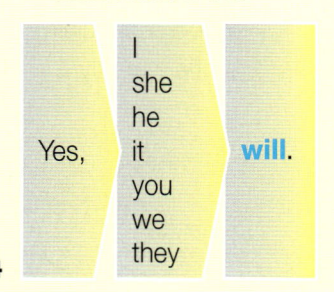

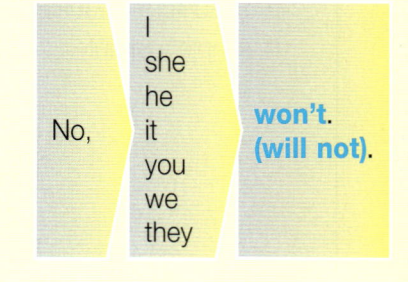

Yes, I / she / he / it / you / we / they **will**.

No, I / she / he / it / you / we / they **won't (will not)**.

8 We shouldn't waste energy

1b   1 bad   2 good   3 bad   4 good

2a

People use wood — to heat their homes.
People save energy — to stop pollution.
Some people take showers — to save hot water.

b   Some countries **use** the wind **to make** energy.
The first verb (*use*) = the action.
The second verb (*to + make*) = the purpose (making energy).

Use *to* + base form to talk about the purpose of actions.

The first verb can be different forms/tenses, but the second verb is always *to* + base form.

4a
- \+ We **should** take showers.
- – We **shouldn't** travel by car.
- ? **Should** we save energy?
  What **should** we do?

b
- \+ I should save energy.
- – They shouldn't waste energy.
- ? Should we take baths?
  How should we travel?

---

should

affirmative

I / She / He / It / You / We / They   **should**   stop.

negative

I / She / He / It / You / We / They   **shouldn't (should not)**   stop.

questions

Should   I / she / he / it / you / we / they   stop?

What / When / Who / Why / Where / How   **should**   I / she / he / it / you / we / they   stop?

Use *should*
- to give answers to problems:
  We should stop pollution.
- to talk about rules:
  She shouldn't walk on the grass.
- to give advice to people:
  You are ill. You should go to the doctor.

short answers

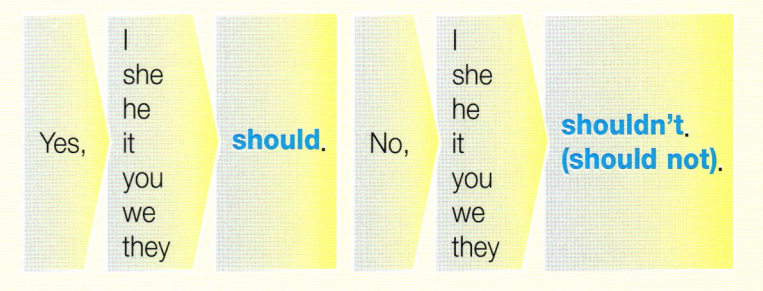

Yes, I / she / he / it / you / we / they **should**.   No, I / she / he / it / you / we / they **shouldn't (should not)**.

9 Are you doing anything next Saturday?

1b 1 future   2 future

Use the present continuous (and *going to*) to talk about future plans.

Use the present continuous to talk about future arrangements.
Example: I'm going to visit Greece. = plan.
I'm visiting Greece. = I've got a ticket and a hotel. = future arrangement

2

Indefinite pronouns

person	place	thing
somebody (= someone)	somewhere	something
anybody (= anyone)	anywhere	anything
nobody (= no one)	nowhere	nothing
everybody (= everyone)	everywhere	everything

3a
- \+ They're visiting **some**body.
  I'm going **some**where.
- \− I'm not doing **any**thing.
- ? Are you doing **any**thing?

b
- \+ She's doing **some**thing.
- \− We're not meeting **any**body.
  He's not going **any**where.
- ? Is he going **any**where?
  Are you meeting **any**body?

We usually use:

nobody	**some**body	**every**body	
nowhere	**some**where	**every**where	in affirmative
nothing	**some**thing	**every**thing	sentences

anybody	
anywhere	in negative sentences and questions
anything	

10 There aren't enough girls

1b 1 yes   2 yes   3 no
enough – b
too much – c
not enough – a

2a There**'s enough** salad.
There **aren't enough** girls.
There**'s too much** sugar.
There **are too many** boys.

b There **are too many** sandwiches.
There **are not enough** boys.
There **are too many** girls.
There **is not enough** sugar.

Countable and uncountable nouns
We can count some nouns (countable nouns):
one boy, two boys, some boys; one sandwich, two sandwiches, some sandwiches

We can't count other nouns (uncountable nouns):
some salad, some food, some sugar

Use *too many* with countable nouns:
too many boys
Use *too much* with uncountable nouns:
too much sugar

Use *(not) enough* with countable nouns and uncountable nouns.

4a 1 It's too sweet.
2 It's not loud enough.

b 1 It isn't hot enough.   2 It's too hot.
3 It's hot enough.
1 c   2 a   3 b

Put *too* before an adjective: It's **too sweet.**
Put *enough* after the adjective: It isn't **sweet enough.**
It's **sweet enough.**

11 The biggest in the world!

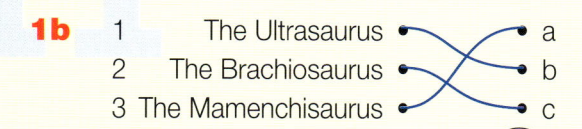

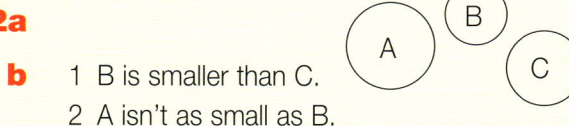

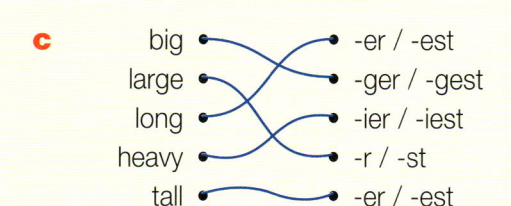

1b
1. The Ultrasaurus — c
2. The Brachiosaurus — a
3. The Mamenchisaurus — b

2a

(A) (B) (C)

b
1. B is smaller than C.
2. A isn't as small as B.

c
- big — -ger / -gest
- large — -r / -st
- long — -er / -est
- heavy — -ier / -iest
- tall — -er / -est

adjective	comparative	superlative
lo**ng**	long**er**	the long**est**
cl**ean**	clean**er**	the clean**est**
b**ig**	bi**gg**er	the bi**gg**est
larg**e**	larg**er**	the larg**est**
heav**y**	heav**ier**	the heav**iest**

Comparative and superlative forms – spelling rules
1 adjective has <u>one syllable</u> and ends in a vowel and then a consonant (e.g. -at, -un, -ig), double – × 2 – the consonant + -er/-est big   + -er   bigger
2 adjective ends in -e, add -r/-st large   + -st   largest
3 adjective has <u>two syllables</u> and ends in -y: ~~y~~ + -ier/-iest heavy   + -ier   heavier happy   + -iest   happiest
But: adjective ends in -w, -y or -x, do <u>not</u> double the consonant new   + -er   newer 4 adjective ends in two or more consonants or ends in two or more vowels and then one consonant, add -er/-est longer   + -er   longer clean   + -est   cleanest

12 It's the best!

1
Black Swan	** – ****
Sunlaws House	*****

2
beautiful	3	exciting	3
expensive	3	far	1
friendly	2	interesting	3 (4)
peaceful	2	quiet	2
romantic	3	small	1

Rules	

1 Don't use *more* and *most* with adjectives with 1 syllable:
   long → longer → longest
   clean → cleaner → cleanest
	4 Don't use *more* and *most* with some adjectives with 2 syllables
	   clever → cleverer → cleverest
	   quiet → quieter → quietest

2 Use *more* and *most* with adjectives with 2 syllables:
   peaceful → more peaceful → most peaceful
   boring → more boring → most boring
	5 Use *more* and *most* with adjectives with 3+ syllables:
	   expensive → more expensive → most expensive
	   intelligent → more intelligent → most intelligent

3 Don't use *more* and *most* with adjectives with 2 syllables with -y at the end:
   easy → easier → easiest
   happy → happier → happiest
	6 ⚠ No rule!
	   bad → worse → worst
	   far → further / farther → furthest / farthest
	   good → better → best

13 It was rising from the sea

1b 1 past   2 no   3 an island

2a + They **were** look**ing** at a new island.
  − They **weren't** look**ing** at a boat.

While they were fishing, they saw something.
They were sailing nearer when it suddenly grew larger.

b + They **were** sail**ing** in the Atlantic.
  − The island **wasn't** grow**ing** smaller.

They were fishing when they saw something.
While they were sailing nearer, it grew larger.

Past continuous

affirmative

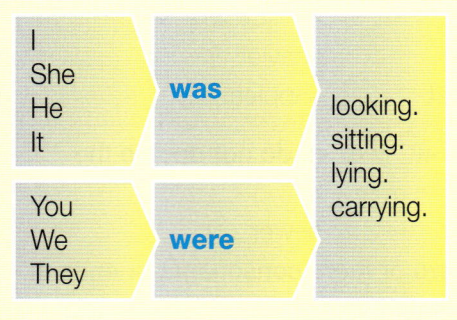

| I / She / He / It | was | looking. sitting. lying. carrying. |
| You / We / They | were | |

negative

| I / She / He / It | wasn't (was not) | looking. sitting. lying. carrying. |
| You / We / They | weren't (were not) | |

Use the past continuous to talk about an action/event at a time in the past:

- the action / event started before the time, and it continued after the time.
  At one o'clock, I was having lunch.

- another action / event (in the past simple) stopped or changed the first action / event.
  While I was walking in the park, a dog bit me!
  I was walking in the park when a dog bit me!

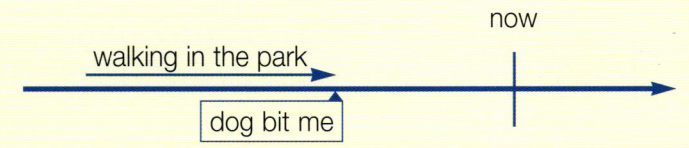

Use *while* with the past continuous part of the sentence OR use *when* with the past simple part of the sentence. With *while*, put a comma (,) after the past continuous part of the sentence.

14 Which one was driving?

1b 1 F 2 T

2a
1 **Where were** you stand**ing**? — Next to the telephones.
2 **Who was** driv**ing**? — The short man.
3 **Was** he driv**ing** fast? — Yes, he was.

b
1 **Who** was stand**ing** next to the telephones? — Sue.
2 **Were** the men speak**ing** quietly to the bus driver? — No, they weren't.
3 **What were** they argu**ing** about? — The accident.

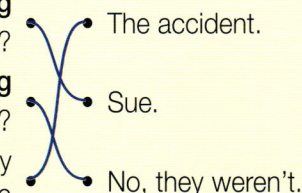

Past continuous

questions

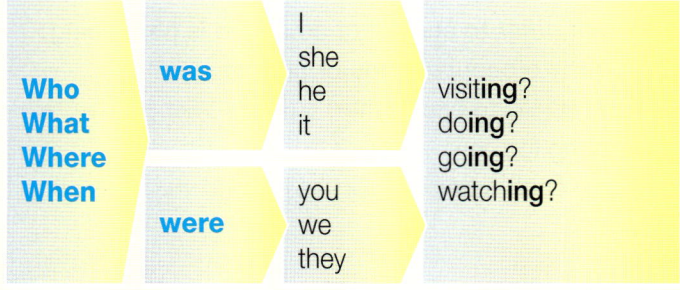

| Was | I / she / he / it | driving? standing? |
| Were | you / we / they | |

| Who / What / Where / When | was | I / she / he / it | visiting? doing? going? watching? |
| | were | you / we / they | |

short answers

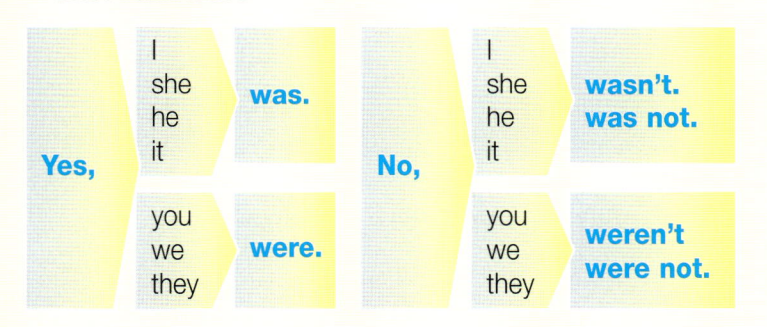

| Yes, | I / she / he / it | was. |
| | you / we / they | were. |

| No, | I / she / he / it | wasn't. was not. |
| | you / we / they | weren't. were not. |

4a 1 one   2 ones   3 ones   4 one

b 1 Which, one
2 Which, ones

one = a singular countable noun.
He was wearing **a jumper**. It was a red **one**.
ones = plural countable noun.
She was standing next to **the phones** – the new **ones**.

Use *Which* for asking about a thing/things or a person/people from a small groups of things/people. We know all the things/people in the group:
Which car was he driving? = I can see three cars. He was driving one of these cars.
Which phones are new? = There are two groups of phones. One group is new.

We often use *Which* in questions with *one* or *ones*.
A man hit the bus driver. **Which one?**

What do you want?
I want a pen.
Which one/pen do you want?
I want the red **one**.

15 He is the pilot that built the smallest plane

1b 1 T   2 F   3 T

2a 1 He is the pilot that built the smallest plane.
2 *Concorde* is a passenger plane that can fly at 2,300 kilometres an hour.

b 1 Bumble Bee is a plane that is only 2.6 metres long.
2 The Wright brothers were the pilots that flew the first plane.

You can use *that* for people and things.

4a 1 Orville and Wilbur Wright were <u>brothers</u> **who** invented the aeroplane
2 They built <u>an aeroplane</u> **which** flew 36.5 metres.

b 1 Robert H Starr is <u>the man</u> **who** flew the smallest plane.
2 *Concorde* is <u>a plane</u> **which** carries passengers.

c

| that | person | who |
| that | thing | which |

Use *which* (or *that*) for things. Use *who* (or *that*) for people.

16 I really enjoyed myself

1b 1 T 2 F

2

object pronouns	reflexive pronouns
me	myself
you (😊)	yourself
him	himself
her	herself
it	itself
we	ourselves
you (😊😊+)	yourselves
them	themselves

3 1 b 2 c 3 a

Use reflexive / emphatic pronouns
- to show that the subject and the object are the same:
  We saw **ourselves** on video.
- to mean 'alone' or 'without help':
  I did my homework **myself**.

Use *each other* to show that an action is happening between two people/things or groups:
They are talking to **each other**. = She is talking to him and he is talking to her.
They love **each other**. = He loves her and she loves him.

17 I used to forget everything!

1b 1 F 2 T 3 T 4 F

2a
+ I **used to** forget everything!
− I **didn't use to** enjoy it.
? **Did** you **use to** enjoy school?
  What **did** you **use to** forget?

c Studying used to be a problem. – b

b
+ Carol **used to** hate studying.
− She **didn't use to** remember things.
? **Did** she **use to** forget names?
  What **did** she **use to** hate?

Used to

affirmative and negative

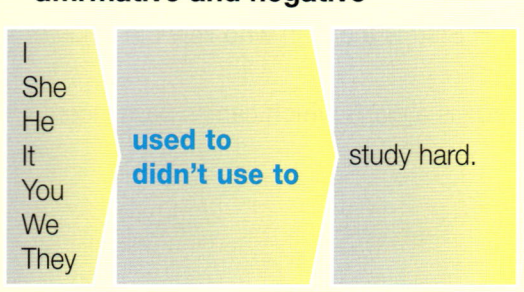

I She He It You We They	used to / didn't use to	study hard.

questions

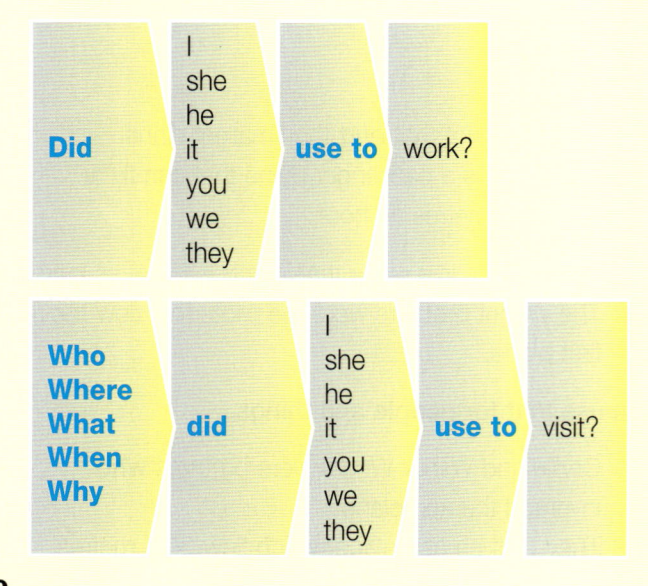

Did	I she he it you we they	use to	work?

Who Where What When Why	I she he it you we they	did	use to	visit?

short answers

Yes, I/she/he/it/you/we/they **did.**

No, I/she/he/it/you/we/they **didn't.**

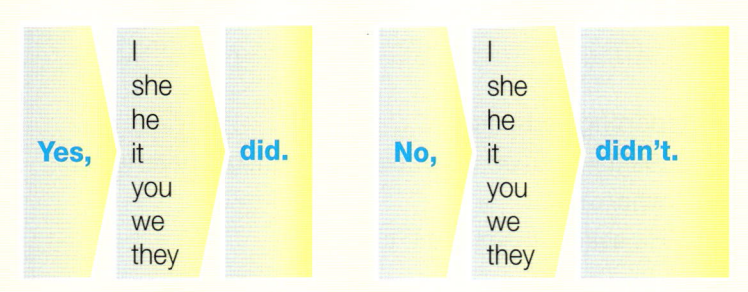

Use *used to* for
- things that you usually did in the past but don't do now
- things that were true in the past but are not true now
- things that usually happened in the past but don't happen now

18 I won't be able to live without you

1b last week = b   now = a   next week = c

b

2a
+ You **could smell** the Bad Brothers from 200 metres.
− He **couldn't catch** them.
? **Will** he **be able to** walk?
   Yes, he **will**. He**'ll be able to** run.

	could	will be able to
+	He **could** do it.	He**'ll be able to** do it.
−	He **couldn't** do it.	He **won't be able to** do it.
?	**Could** he do it?	**Will** he **be able to** do it?

Past *could*

affirmative and negative

I/She/He/It/You/We/They **could** / **couldn't** do it.

questions

Could I/she/he/it/you/we/they do it?

short answers

Yes, I/she/he/it/you/we/they **could.**

No, I/she/he/it/you/we/they **couldn't.**

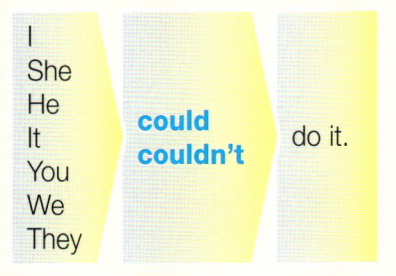

Future *will be able to*

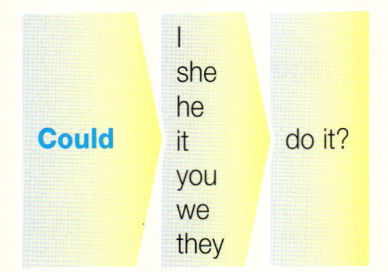

affirmative and negative

I/She/He/It/You/We/They **will be able to** / **won't be able to** do it.

questions

Will I/she/he/it/you/we/they **be able to** do it?

short answers

Yes, I/she/he/it/you/we/they **will.**

No, I/she/he/it/you/we/they **won't.**

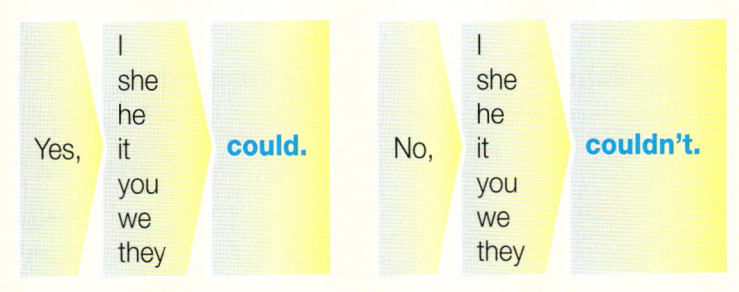

Use *can / could / will be able to* to talk about ability:
She can do it. = She <u>is</u> able to do it in the present.

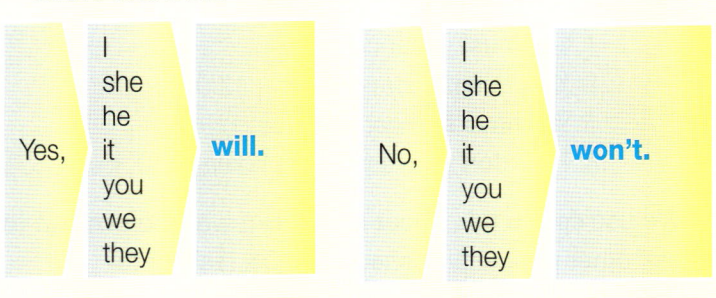

She could do it. = She <u>was</u> able to do it in the past.
She will be able to do it in the future.

19 Smith asked her where the robot was

1b 1 ✓ 2 ✓ 3 ✗

2a 1 I **can't tell you**.
2 She said that **they were secret**.
3 The plans **are for a robot**.
4 **I said that I was looking for the plans**.

Reported speech
To speak about something which someone said, **change present tenses to past tenses.**

b 1 said   2 told   3 told   4 said

Reporting verbs: say, tell
- We <u>say</u> something (to someone).
  He **said that** she **could** see.
- We <u>tell</u> someone (about something/someone).
  He **told them** (**that** she **could** see).
- We usually put *that* after *say* or *tell*, but sometimes we don't.

4 1 **Where are the plans?**
2 I asked **her if she knew Professor X.**
3 **Where is the robot?**
4 Smith asked **if it was dangerous.**

Reporting verb: ask
- We <u>ask</u> (someone) **if/how/what/when/where/which/who/why …**
  He **asked** (them) **if** she **could** see.

Direct speech
Use speech marks (' ') to write someone's words.
Don't change the person's words.

20 You must come home at 10.30

1b 1 yes   2 no   3 5 o'clock

2a 1 = ability   2 = permission
b 1 no   2 no
c 1 no   2 yes

3a 1 You **must** come home at 10.30.
2 You **mustn't** be late.
3 You **have to** get up early.
4 They **don't have to** get up at 5 o'clock.

b 1 You **must** get enough sleep.
2 You **mustn't** come home at 12.00.
3 You **have to** meet your granddad.
4 They **don't have to** come home at 10.30.

We use *can* to talk about ability. But we also use *can* to ask other people and check it is OK (asking for permission) before we do things:
Can I use your computer, please?

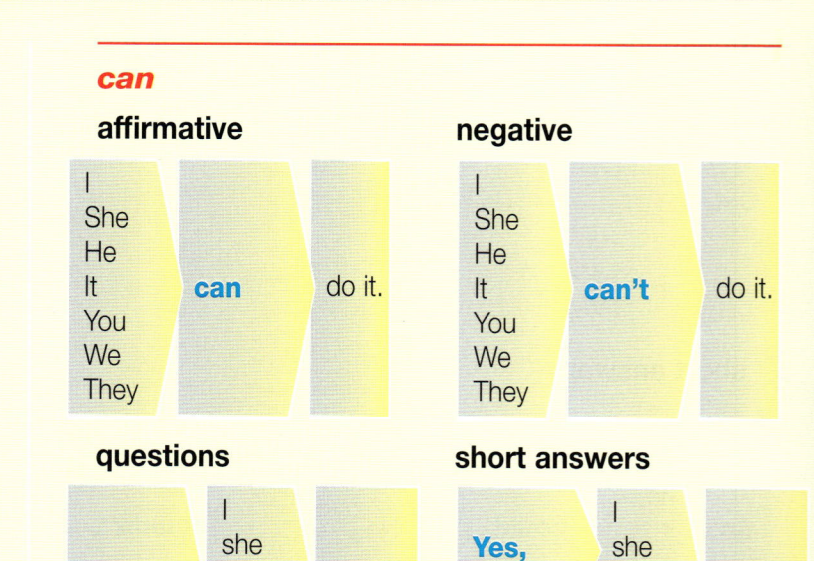

can

affirmative

| I / She / He / It / You / We / They | **can** | do it. |

negative

| I / She / He / It / You / We / They | **can't** | do it. |

questions

| **Can** | I / she / he / it / you / we / they | do it? |

short answers

| **Yes,** | I / she / he / it / you / we / they | **can.** |
| **No,** | | **can't.** |

We use *must* and *have to* to talk about things we can't choose or decide about for ourselves. For example, rules:
You **must** take the library books back to the library.
She **has to** wear a school uniform.

We also use *mustn't* in the same way:
You **mustn't** steal.

But *don't have to* is different:
She **doesn't have to** stay in. = She can stay in or she can go out. She can choose.

We use *can* (for permission), *must* and *have to* to talk about the present and the future, not the past.

must

affirmative

I / She / He / It / You / We / They **must** do it.

negative

I / She / He / It / You / We / They **mustn't** do it.

have to

affirmative

I / We / You / They **have to** do it.

She / He / It **has to** do it.

negative

I / We / You / They **don't have to** do it.

She / He / It **doesn't have to** do it.

21 The work has been hard

1b 1 5   2 no   3 no

2

infinitive	past simple	past participle
be	was/were	**been**
build	built	**built**
do	did	**done**
give	gave	**given**
see	saw	**seen**
start	started	**started**
take	took	**taken**

The past participle form for regular verbs is the same as the past simple, for example:
finished – finished.
Verbs with irregular past simple forms have irregular past participles too.
Use the past participle to make the present perfect simple.
Use the present perfect simple to talk about actions in the past which change things in the present.

I'**ve broken** my leg. – I can't walk.
I **broke** my leg. – But it's OK now.

Past participles
irregular verbs

be	was/were	**been**	get	got	**got**	sit	sat	**sat**
begin	began	**begun**	give	gave	**given**	sleep	slept	**slept**
break	broke	**broken**	go	went	**gone**	smell	smelled	**smelled**
bring	brought	**brought**	grow	grew	**grown**		smelt	**smelt**
build	built	**built**	have	had	**had**	speak	spoke	**spoken**
buy	bought	**bought**	hear	heard	**heard**	spend	spent	**spent**
catch	caught	**caught**	hit	hit	**hit**	stand	stood	**stood**
come	came	**come**	keep	kept	**kept**	steal	stole	**stolen**
cost	cost	**cost**	know	knew	**known**	swim	swam	**swum**
cut	cut	**cut**	learn	learned	**learned**	take	took	**taken**
do	did	**done**		learnt	**learnt**	teach	taught	**taught**
draw	drew	**drawn**	make	made	**made**	tell	told	**told**
drink	drank	**drunk**	mean	meant	**meant**	think	thought	**thought**
drive	drove	**driven**	meet	met	**met**	throw	threw	**thrown**
eat	ate	**eaten**	put	put	**put**	understand	understood	**understood**
fall	fell	**fallen**	read	read	**read**	wake	woke	**woken**
feed	fed	**fed**	ride	rode	**ridden**	wear	wore	**worn**
find	found	**found**	run	ran	**run**	win	won	**won**
fly	flew	**flown**	see	saw	**seen**	write	wrote	**written**
forget	forgot	**forgotten**	sing	sang	**sung**			

3a
+ The villagers **have done** the work.
+ The work **has been** hard.
− The people **haven't built** a well.

b
+ The people in Anoma's village **have built** a well.
− The work **hasn't been** easy.

5a 1 b   2 c   3 a
b   1 b   2 c   3 a

With the present perfect simple:
- Use *just* for something that happened a very short time ago.
- Use *already* for things further in the past. We often use *already* to show that an action has finished early.
- Use *yet* in negative sentences to talk about things that are going to happen but haven't happened.
- We usually put *just* and *already* after *have/has* and before the past participle. We usually put *yet* at the end of the sentence:
  I've **just** done it.   I've **already** done it.
  I haven't done it **yet**.

Present perfect simple
affirmative

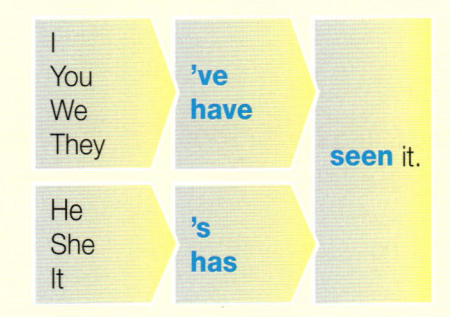

| I You We They | **'ve** **have** | |
| He She It | **'s** **has** | **seen** it. |

negative

| I You We They | **haven't** **have not** | |
| She He It | **hasn't** **has not** | **seen** it. |

74

22 Where have you put the chocolates?

1b 1 T 2 T 3 F

2a
1 Have you finished your homework?
2 Yes, I have.
3 Where have you put the chocolates?

b
1 **Have** Elena and Kim **finished** their homework?
2 Yes, **they have**.
3 **Who has eaten** the chocolates?
   Liam has!

Present perfect simple

questions

| Have | I/you/we/they | finished? |
| Has | she/he/it | |

| Who/What/Where | have | I/you/we/they | visited? |
| | has | she/he/it | |

short answers

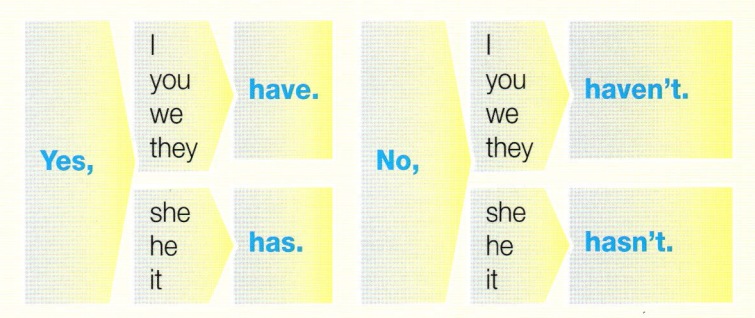

Yes, I/you/we/they **have.** / she/he/it **has.**
No, I/you/we/they **haven't.** / she/he/it **hasn't.**

4a
1 Have you **ever** been to Brazil?
2 I've **never** been to a foreign country.

b
1 Have you **ever** eaten Paulo's cooking?
2 I've **never** eaten Brazilian food.

c 1 a 2 b

be/go
He's **been** to Scotland. = He went and came home.
He's **gone** to Scotland. = He's in Scotland now.
Use *be* not *go* to talk about visits in the present perfect:
He's **been** to Scotland every year.
(He'll **go** to Scotland next year.
He **goes** to Scotland every year.)

Use present perfect simple questions to ask about actions in the past that change things in the present. Use *ever* with present perfect simple questions to ask about things that we have done at any time in our lives. Use the past simple to ask and answer questions about the time of actions in the past.

23 If he isn't fit, he won't play in the big match

1b 1 yes 2 don't know 3 no 4 don't know

2a
1 They'll play Chelsea **if** they win.
2 **If** he isn't fit**,** he won't play.

b
1 Derby **will** keep the trophy **if** they win the final.
2 **If** Stoke win tomorrow, they **will play** Chelsea next week.
3 **If** Stoke don't win tomorrow, they **won't play** Chelsea next week.

c future

First conditional
Use the first conditional to talk about pairs of actions or events in the future. But we <u>don't know</u> that the first action or event will happen.
We use *if* + the present simple to talk about the first action or event, and the future simple to talk about the second action or event.

- *if* + present simple + comma (,)   +   future simple (*will/won't* + infinitive)

| If | it **rains**, | I**'ll stay** in. |
| If | it **doesn't rain**, | I **won't stay** in. |

- future simple   +   *if* + present simple

| I**'ll stay** in | if | it **rains**. |
| I **won't stay** in | if | it **doesn't rain**. |

24 Honey is eaten everywhere

1b 1 The workers.   2 The workers.
   3 Karl von Frisch.

2a 1 Honey Bees **are kept** by farmers.
   2 Honey **is made** by the worker bees.
   3 Their dance **was written** about by Karl von Frisch.

b 1 The drones **are chased** by the workers.
   2 The work **is done** by the workers.
   3 Bees **were studied** by Karl von Frisch.

Passive
active = The dog **bit** the queen.
passive = The queen **was bitten** by the dog.

Present simple passive
= present simple of *be* + past participle

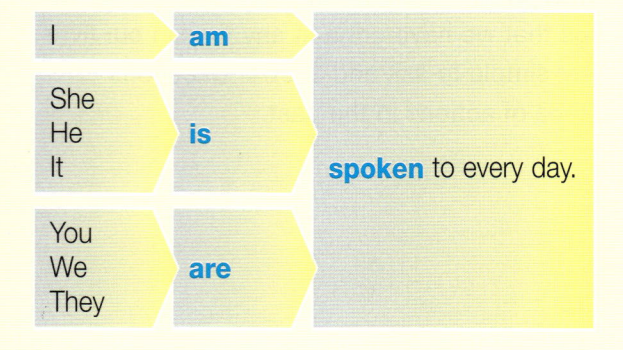

I	**am**	
She / He / It	**is**	**spoken** to every day.
You / We / They	**are**	

Use the passive
- when we don't know who does/did the action:
My bag **was stolen**. (= someone stole my bag. I don't know who.)
- when the action or the person/thing it happens to is more interesting/important than the person/thing who does it:
Bees **are kept** by farmers.
The queen **was bitten** by a dog.

Use *by* to talk about the person/thing that does/did the action.

Past simple passive
= past simple of *be* + past participle

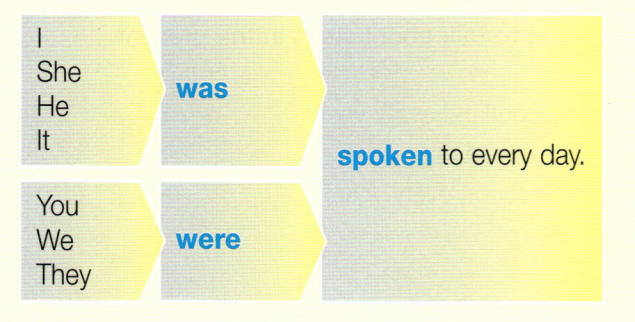

I / She / He / It	**was**	
		spoken to every day.
You / We / They	**were**	

5a 1 They do **a** dance. **The** dance tells the other workers where to look.
   2 They live together in **a** hive. **The** hive is built by the workers.

b 1 Every hive has got **a** queen. **The** queen is fed by the workers.
   2 Karl von Frisch wrote **a** book. **The** book is about bees.

c We use *a/an* to talk about a singular countable noun for the first time. People don't know which thing you are talking about.
We use *the* to talk about the same thing again because people know which thing you are talking about.

Wordlist

Write the meanings or other notes for the words below

n = noun
v = verb
adj = adjective
adv = adverb

Meaning | Meaning | Meaning

a

ability 18
accident 14
agree 4
air 7
all 8
argue 3
arrive 9
art 3
artist 2
astronaut 7
away 2

b

badly 5
balloon 15
band 3
basin 17
bath 8
bead 21
bee 24
begin 2
believe 4
best 12
better 12
bicycle 14
biology 3
bite 3
bone 4
boring 6
bravely 5

bring 7
bucket 10
build 4
building 18
bus driver 14
busily 5
buy 3

c

camp 6
careful 5
carefully 5
castle 12
cause 8
cave 17
chase 2
cheap 12
cheese 10
cheetah 5
chocolate 22
clearly 17
close (v) 8
coal 8
comfortable 5
comfortably 5
corn 4
countryside 6
cross (v) 14
cry 2
cut 3
cycle 6

d

dangerously 5
day 5
difficult 6
dinosaur 11
distance 13
dive 6
drone 24
dye 3

e

eagle 5
Earth 4
easily 5
easy 5
eater 5
electricity 8
energy 8
enough 10
ever 22
everybody 9
everyone 9
everything 9
everywhere 9
exam 23
exercise 6

f

farm 1
feed 16
final 23
fingernail 3

77

Meaning	Meaning	Meaning
fisherman 13	honey 24	monster 13
flower 24	hospital 19	most 8
food 2	hot dog 17	museum 4
football match 16	hotel 12	musician 3
footprint 14		
forget 3	**i**	**n**
France 22	idea 6	near 13
fun 6	important 6	New Year 3
further 12	inside 7	nice 11
furthest 12	intelligent 12	night 5
	interpreter 3	noisily 5
g		noisy 5
gas 8	**j**	
gate 8	jogging 6	**o**
gentle 5	jumper 10	omelette 10
gently 5	junk food 3	on foot 17
get 3	just 21	on time 23
ghost 12		onion 10
giraffe 11	**k**	orange (adj) 14
glass 8	king 24	outside 7
goat 8		owl 5
ground 17	**l**	
guide book 4	large 11	**p**
	leisure activities 6	painter 2
h	library 20	painting 2
hamburger 20	light (n) 8	parrot 15
hamster 1	literature 3	pass 23
happen 2	look at 2	passenger 12
happily 5	loud 5	patient (adj) 5
hard 5	loudly 5	patiently 5
healthy 3		pay 16
heat 8	**m**	peaceful 12
helicopter 15	mammoth 17	pepper 10
hit 14	meal 6	perhaps 7
hive 24	mirror 16	permission 20
hobby 6	money 4	phone 14
	monkey 5	

	Meaning
physics 3	
pilot 15	
plan 18	
plane 15	
player 23	
point 16	
police officer 14	
polite 12	
pollution 8	
present (n) 3	
pyramid 24	

q

queen 24	
quiet 5	
quietly 5	

r

rabbit 1	
rebuild 18	
recycle 8	
red 14	
regularly 6	
remember 14	
repair 16	
resolution 3	
rider 5	
rise (v) 13	
robot 7	
romantic 12	
round 4	

s

sack 13	
salad 10	
salt 10	

	Meaning
save 7	
seat belt 14	
secret 9	
semi-final 23	
send 7	
shape 22	
shell 4	
ship 2	
shower 8	
sightseeing 6	
silent 5	
silently 5	
simple 5	
simply 5	
ski 22	
skin 17	
slowly 5	
smoke 6	
snake 5	
space station 7	
spaceship 7	
Spain 4	
specially 5	
spend 20	
steal 18	
strange 5	
submarine 15	
sweet (adj) 4	
sweet potato 4	

t

tap (n) 8	
tap dancer 17	
tape (n) 16	
teach 1	

	Meaning
team 23	
tell 18	
terribly 5	
themselves 16	
tomato 10	
tool 4	
tortoise 5	
town 4	
traffic lights 14	
travel 4	
trophy 23	
turn off 8	
turn up 10	
twins 18	
type 24	

v

vehicle 15	
vet 18	
villager 21	

w

waste 8	
wave 2	
well (adv) 5	
well (n) 21	
wheel 15	
wind 8	
wing 15	
wood 4	
work 2	
worker 5	
worse 12	
worst 12	

y

yellow 14	

Thanks and acknowledgements

I would especially like to thank the editorial team at Cambridge University Press, in particular Jeanne McCarten, Nóirín Burke, Bella Wigan and Liz Driscoll for their encouragement, patience and invaluable help. I would also like to thank the design team, especially Marcus Askwith and Samantha Dumiak, for their astonishing creativity. Finally, a deeply heartfelt thanks to Alison Sharpe for all her support and sensitivity when most needed.

Many thanks also to the following teachers, students and institutions from all over the world who reviewed and pilot tested material from *Grammar Works 2*: Carlos Barbisan, São Paulo, Brazil; Sarah Brierley, Cambridge, UK; Doukas School, Maroussi, Greece; Simon J Himbury, Hilderstone College Tokyo, Tokyo, Japan; Fumimasa Ishigu, The Attached High School to Hiroshima University, Hiroshima, Japan; Grazyna Kanska, Warsaw, Poland; Zsuzsa Kuti and Judit Szepesi, Budapesti Tantiokepzo Foiskola Gyakorlo Iskolaje, Budapest, Hungary; Nigel Moore, Akita National College of Technology, Akita City, Japan; Caroline Nixon, 'Star English', Murcia, Spain; Marcela del Pilar Naveas López, Santiago, Chile; Anna Sikorzynska, Warsaw, Poland; Wayne Trotman, Özel Cakabey Koleji, Izmir, Turkey; H Tuta Sonbay, Özel Tarahan Lisesi, Istanbul, Turkey.

Mick Gammidge, June 1998.

The publishers are grateful to the following for permission to reproduce copyright material. It has not always been possible to identify the sources of all the material used and in such cases the publishers would welcome information from the copyright owners.

For permission to reproduce photographs and other copyright material:

Tate Gallery, London 1998 for page 6, *The Last of England* by Ford Madox Brown; Mansell/Time Inc./Katz for page 10, Columbus landing; Hodder & Stoughton Educational for pages 10 and 11, texts adapted from *World Travellers and Explorers* by Derek Merrill; Erica Echenberg Redferns for page 16, Lee Murray; NASA/Science Photo Library for page 18, Sojourner on Mars and for page 19, space walk; Angela Hampton/Euroscene for page 21, recycling; courtesy of the Black Swan Hotel for page 28, The Black Swan Hotel; courtesy of The Sunlaws House Hotel for page 28, The Sunlaws House Hotel; The Scottish Borders Tourist Board for page 28, The Borders; courtesy of National Motor Museum, Beaulieu for page 29, Porsche; B. Masters/Quadrant for page 29, Ford T; Flight International/Quadrant for page 36, Wright brothers and Boeing 747; R. Shaw/Quadrant for page 36, Concorde; photo by R. H. Starr for page 36, Bumble Bee; Ron Giling/Panos for page 50, water project; Oxford Scientific Films for page 56, bees; Scott Camazine/Oxford Scientific Films for page 56, wild hive; Alastair Shay/Oxford Scientific Films for page 56, queen bee; Konrad Wotha/Oxford Scientific Films for page 56, bee on flower; Louvre, Paris/Bridgeman Art Library, London & New York for page 57, Mona Lisa; Michael Holford for page 57, pyramids; Greenwich Royal Observatory/Science Photo Library for page 57, telescope; Jim Holmes/Panos Pictures for page 57, rice farmer.

We would like to thank the following for pictures taken on commission for Cambridge University Press:

Jeremy Pembrey for page 5, girl with rabbit; Nigel Luckhurst for page 40, graduate.

Illustrations:

Gerry Ball, Phil Burrows, Madeleine Hardy, Phil Healey, David Mitcheson, Peter Richardson, Jamie Sneddon, Sam Thompson, Kath Walker, Celia Witchard.

Produced by Gecko Limited, Bicester, Oxon